DOWN THE
ROAD AND
ROUND THE
BEND

To Elaine, naturally...

On any road, a journey is halved in good company, in a loving relationship, it flies.

If years were miles, then, hopefully, we are about to clock 50, pothole free.

Down the Road and Round the Bend
Published in Great Britain in 2018
by Graffeg Limited

Written by Roy Noble copyright © 2018.
Designed and produced by Graffeg Limited copyright © 2018.

Graffeg Limited, 24 Stradey Park Business Centre,
Mwrwg Road, Llangennech, Llanelli,
Carmarthenshire SA14 8YP Wales UK
Tel 01554 824000 www.graffeg.com

ISBN 9781912050178

1 2 3 4 5 6 7 8 9

DOWN THE ROAD AND ROUND THE BEND

Roy Noble

GRAFFEG

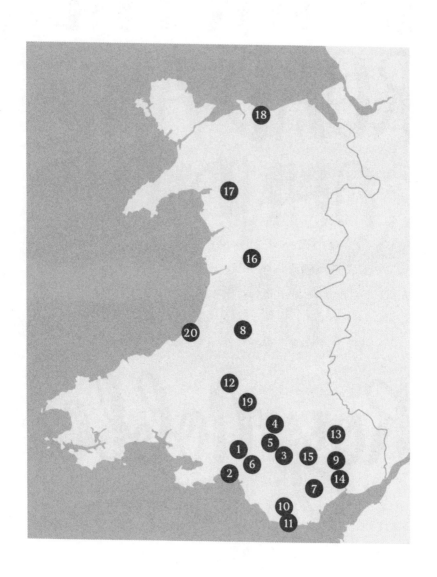

Contents

Preface

I once felt deep jealousy when speaking to a man in the far west seaside village of Sneem, in the Kingdom of Kerry, Ireland. Like me, he had been the headteacher of a village school, but he had decided to give up that laudable, worthy and soul-warming post to become a full-time storyteller. In Ireland they are called a *Seanchal*; a near English pronunciation is 'shanachie'.

This man had stories that lasted twenty seconds and stories that lasted twenty minutes. He would travel the world visiting communities of the Irish diaspora. For added atmosphere and effect he'd sometimes wear a waistcoat and put on a hat, but what a job. You could sense the fulfilment in the aura about him.

Storytelling has been a joy for me, in schools and in groups and gatherings. Oral tales passed down the generations are the lifeblood of heritage, for families, for tribes, for communities, for countries. I regret deeply that, in our modern day, there is an endangered species... aunties. They were the ones who seemed to know all the details and pass them on.

Oral tales have given way, in most part, but not entirely, thankfully, to the written word. Hence, this book. It is a rambling compendium of 'tales from Wales' – fact, fiction and fanciful. I say rambling because in each chapter there is a story from a particular patch on the quilt that is Wales, but each main tale rolls on to others nearby, from almost the same map grid lines. My subject is geography, but my passion is history, both members of a close family of studies. Some are well-known mythological tales from beyond the far-distant horizon, others are close, personal stories of places I have been and events that have happened. Many are so near that you might not really have thought twice about them, they are 'just down the road and 'round the bend', and they are part of who and what you are.

The stories here have all intrigued me. Is it true that on the ridge above Rhigos, if you turn east, the next highest point is in the Urals of Russia? Was the first red flag of insurrection in history actually flown on Hirwaun Common? It can't be true that Napoleon actually spent a night in the Castle Hotel, Neath, can it?

There are definite truths, of course, like the explosion at the Universal coal mine at Senghenydd in 1913, it being the largest, deadliest coal mine disaster in Britain. Go to Banwen and seek out the monument on which is written 'St. Patrick was born here' and believe it...go on. Receive a toast of good health from Tredegar, where the National Health Service came into being when Aneurin Bevan wanted to Tredegarise Britain.

Will they ever get serious about finding the lost elephant of Tregaron? If you have an orthopaedic problem, why not try the Holy Well at Patrishow, in the back hills of Abergavenny and Crickhowell.

On the transport ley line that is the A470, did you know that south of Merthyr Tydfil you actually drive through the infamous mud and spoil heap avalanche that engulfed Pantglas School and a street in Aberfan in 1966? Further north, passing the reservoirs as you head for the Storey Arms and the Brecon Beacons, does one ever give a thought for the two hamlets that lie beneath the Llwyn Onn water?

Moulded into the storytelling is the fabled saga of

the Maid of Cefn Ydfa in the Llynfi Valley, a sad story of unrequited love. If you fancy yourself a poet, get confirmation on Cadair Idris, above Dolgellau, but take care, for spending a night there could result in side-effects... If you fancy your chances, 'there's gold in them thar hills', as shouted out by the panners of the Real Wild West.

Poetry also takes us to Trawsfynydd, the home of the tragic poet Heddwyn, killed on the first day of the Battle of Passcendaele before he won the Chair at the National Eisteddfod. On the horizon of his homeland stands a sombre image of the *Quatermass* television series, a nuclear energy reactor.

There is Llanwonno and its connection with both Guto Nŷth Bran and the Zulus who fought the film stars Stanley Baker and Michael Cain. On the military front, is it true that a missing recruiting sergeant actually forms part of the wider wall at the pub in Penderyn? What of the grotto and the folly, in Pontypool, and the hamlet of British in the same valley?

Learn of the 'coffin trail' on the Black Mountain, the *cwtch* blanket en-route, the Coed y Bleiddiau cottage's connection with a Russian spy and Lord Haw-Haw, propaganda broadcaster of World War Two, near the slate capital of Blaenau Ffestiniog. Beyond beautiful Betws-y-Coed, with a busy ghost in one hotel and a shoe-throwing ghost in one of its shops, is a small town that sought a seat on the United Nations Security Council as an independent state within Wales. Then we come to an alligator and an elephant in Port Wrexham, and where is Port Wrexham, by the way?

Among all of these lay-bys on the trail, Llewelyn the Last, Arthur's last battle, the Lady of the Lake, the pealing bells of a sunken town and Caradog all get their space. Add the Alamo connection to Dinas in the west, an air disaster in Llandow, a visiting enemy U-boat calling to get butter, eggs and milk during wartime, an uncle who had one leg but three wives and the finished mural contains, hopefully, a range of quite colourful landscapes and portraits.

I hope the brush strokes meet with your approval.

1. Banwen... begorrah!

Port Talbot

It is said that the world is divided into two kinds of people, those who do, and those who get the credit for it.

I would say that the world is divided into three kinds of people: those who make things happen, those who watch things happen and those who ask, 'What's happening then?'

You need the doers as well as the dreamers, because the doers put the rivets in dreams to bring them to fruition. Sometimes it needs persistence and commitment, because commitment will find a way, indifference will find an excuse. Positive thinking, that's also a good engine for progress.

Julius Caesar displayed positive thinking when he first came to Britain in 55 B.C. It is said that he jumped off the boat on the south-east coast of England, tripped and fell on to the beach, but grabbing a fist full of sand, jumped up and shouted, 'Veni, Vidi, Vici.' I came, I saw, I conquered. Good upbeat thinking, but not very effective; all he acquired was a bit of beach. He went back to Gaul, but not to be outdone, he came again in 54 B.C. I wonder if he edited his script a little and, possibly, on landing and keeping his footing, shouted out, 'Veni, Vidi, Velcro.' I came, I saw, and I stuck to it.

The tale unfolding here has a Roman touch to it, in part, and there is a man of the area who is ardently 'sticking to it', to being a dreamer and a doer. His vision, his story, his passion, is encapsulated in a stone. A standing stone.

To be fair, the standing stone should be three times the height. It marks the place where a saint was born. Not an ordinary, third division, run-of-the-mill saint of limited responsibility, but a premier division saint, a patron saint. It stands on the wild, wet, and raw moorland that separates the Upper Swansea Valley from the Neath Valley, near the spot where the Glynneath to Abercrave main road crosses Sarn Helen, the Roman road, on its marching journey from Roman Nidum, Neath, to Y Gaer, near Brecon, and onwards towards Deva Victrix, Chester. A quarter of a mile from the crossroads, travelling north alongside the Sarn Helen, are to be found the remains of Ricus, a Roman fort at Coelbren, and nearer, quietly unnoticed in a stretch of bog, is a large Roman marching camp. Both Roman bus stops are best seen when snow lies on the ground and past walls and edging ditches are lined across the white landscape. The Romans came, allegedly, because the area was rich in iron deposits and all iron production in the Roman Empire was under military jurisdiction.

On my frequent journeys across this moorland from Brynaman to Aberdare, mostly on ardent courting trips in the days of yore and youth, I often mused on the soldiers who were encamped here. Sometimes the mist and drizzling rain added to the atmospheric scene and, on a clear night, when the moon was full above the southern ridge, you could almost sense the ghosts of those who passed that way.

Now, I know that many Roman legions were made up of different nationalities from conquered areas of their empire, but I wonder whether, to supplement numbers, the Romans of their close homeland ever had any kind of National Service for their armed forces, when young

Romans, at the age of eighteen, received 'call-up' papers to join the legions. If they did, I can well imagine some worried Roman mam as she buffed up a brand new breast plate for her boy, asking her Marcus Flavius Junior, 'Where are they sending you, love? Capri, Sicily, the Adriatic? Pompeii, perhaps?' Only to have the vexing reply, 'No, Mam, it's marked here...Banwen, they're sending me to Banwen.'

I bet that the boys who were sent to the outer reaches of the empire were from families of limited means. The well-to-do bucks probably had contacts in the Forum, ensuring that their posting was to the posher suburbs of Rome, or Amalfi, or Portofino, where you could get a Roman chariot day return ticket to get you home. Better still was a Roman doctor's paper declaring you unfit for service.

Serving at Banwen must have been a trial, because the weather there can be damp or the strong moorland breezes render the Roman uniform skirt next to useless. Extra covering had to be thick and *cwtchy* at night. On the other hand, better to be based at Banwen than Pompeii, when you come to think about it. You can knock the climate all you like, but, geologically speaking, there is no volcano in Banwen.

It is said that the marching camp there sometimes had 500 men, having a touch of 'R&R', rest and recuperation for a few days in transit. A sizeable number were cavalry, so little wonder then that on the edge of Banwen the area is still called Maes Marchog to this day: the field of horses, or knights.

Around the fort and the marching camp, a sizeable community grew to serve the needs of the legionnaires. As the years passed and the Roman occupation waned when the empire called them back to defend the homeland, so the area become vulnerable to incursion and sudden attacks. Seaborne raiders, usually from Ireland, called in at Nidum and ventured up the Dulais Valley, pillaging, robbing and kidnapping locals to be used as slaves.

One victim was a young man taken away to be a swineherd. There are various theories about his background; some suggest that his dad was a Roman officer and a deacon. After his kidnapping, life decreed that his presence on the Emerald Isle, his eventual escape and subsequent return was to become a blessing for the western Celts. His religious commitment, in the end, proved saintly. In fact, there was no greater elevation in his gradual promotion than to be dubbed a fully-fledged premier division saint, a patron saint.

That is why the stone in Banwen, bearing the plaque on which is dubbed 'Saint Patrick was born here' should be three times the size. Every 17 March, St Patrick's Day, we gather there to pay him homage. The Vicar comes, the schoolchildren come, and those who believe come. The believers are the ones who are firmly of the view that Patrick was indeed born here. I've checked with scholars of Trinity College Dublin as to the authenticity of the claim and I well remember the encouraging response, delivered in a lilting brogue of charm: 'Well, we know that Patrick was Welsh, we accept that...so if you want to put him down as a Banwen boy, that's fine by us.'

Tomes have been written supporting the theory, some including the purported words of Patrick himself from his death bed, stating that he was a boy of the bog, the marshy moorland of Banavem Taburniae. Banavem...Banwen...at the site of the Taburniae, the tavern, the spot on which a bungalow now stands. Others counter by suggesting that Banavem Taburniae was, in fact, in the Welsh-speaking Kingdom of Strathclyde, Scotland. Even in Wales, his birthplace has been placed in St Davids or the Severn Estuary.

Banwen's more recent history, post Industrial Revolution, centred on iron exploitation and then the quest for coal. Sarn Helen, the Roman road and the area of Maes Marchog featured in the contemporary film *Pride*, which honed in on the miners' strike of 1984-85, when a group of gay activists came down from London to help out and show solidarity.

Deep mining gave way to open-cast mining and these days the turbines of green energy stand as sentries on the hillside, their whirling blades trying to keep in sync and tune with the breeze that comes from the west, sometimes just strong enough to spoil a hairdo and sometimes hurrying on across the moor in coat-closing gusts, heading for Glynneath, Merthyr Tydfil and all points east along the Heads of the Valleys.

In Banwen there lives an extraordinary man, that man of passion and vision that I hinted at earlier. An ex-miner, ex-Far East wartime soldier, author, painter and local historian who lives at the side of Sarn Helen: George Brinley Evans. The figure '90' is carved firmly on his walking stick, a couple of notches down from the top.

Whatever case the other theories put forward, conviction

runs through George's very soul and being, that Patrick, or Padrig was born in Banwen, on the moorland. He has a two-pronged vision, has George. First, he wants the story of Patrick and Banwen cemented and ratified by historians and, secondly, he wants a Premier Inn or Travelodge built in Banwen to cater for all the Irish pilgrims who will want to see where Patrick was born.

And why not? As he says, if they could transform Fatima in Portugal, into a place of 'must-do' pilgrimages after two young girls and a boy saw a vision of the Virgin Mary in 1917, why not Banwen becoming the same kind of magnet? No visions reported yet, as far as we know, but in faith and positive thinking they still might come in droves, following a sacred trail to their patron saint's place of birth. Every 17th March, I'm with George. I'm definitely on his bus of visionary thinking.

2. Castle Gatherings

Neath

Would we have won at Waterloo if Napoleon had not had hemorrhoids? Now that was a puzzling question when it was first thrown at me. Apparently, there is an element of truth in the possibility that Napoleon was having problems 'down below' during the battle; he hadn't been at all well in the days leading up to the conflict and there was a chance that he had been overdoing things on the medical compounds bit.

Why this question struck me again as I was entering Neath Market, you may well ask. In my young days, shopping trips with my mother were usually to Swansea because there was a direct bus route from Brynaman. Neath was the next port of call if the foray to Swansea had been unsuccessful, but the Neath run had to be on another day because it did mean a change of buses at GCG, Gwaun Cae Gurwen. As well as Neath Market, the Neath bus station is held in my memory banks too.

In college years, when I was a student in Cardiff, I changed buses at Neath bus station en-route, changing from the Western Welsh to the faster, limited stop, brown with red stripe, N&C coaches. It was there, on a cold December night, that I met the Angel of Neath Bus Station. I was going home for Christmas, waiting in a queue for the Ammanford bus, via Gwaun Cae Gurwen. There was snow and sleet in the air; it was damp and cold and the gust of a breeze were enough to change your personality. The bus turned up and we all climbed aboard. The bus crew had gone to their canteen for tea and warmth. In no time at all the bus was full, with a few people standing. The last person on was an old man carrying a heavy suitcase, who had rushed from the train to catch his bus connection. Breathless, he took his place in the aisle of the bus.

The two-man crew returned and when the conductor jumped on he counted the standing passengers.

'Sorry,' he said, 'only seven allowed standing and there are eight here, so the last one on will have to get off.'

No one moved, and, fair play, no one pointed to the last one on, the old man. The Christmas spirit was in the air, and anyway, it was cold outside.

'Come on now,' added the conductor. 'Only seven allowed standing, there are eight here, last one on will have to get off.'

No one moved.

'Right,' he said, 'I'm going to get the inspector to sort it out.'

He disappeared and eventually returned with the inspector, who jumped on the bus, counted the standing passengers and shouted, 'Right, this bus is going nowhere unless one gets off...only seven standing, it's in the rules.'

Slowly, the old man picked up his case and shuffled to the steps, got off, and stood at the bus stop in the damp sleet and the very cold air. The conductor was still missing, having stayed in the canteen until it was sorted. The inspector looked at his watch, knocked the window of the driver's cab and shouted, 'Dennis, this bus is late, where's Jack?' With that, the inspector saw another conductor coming out of the canteen. He was a merry looking soul, with mistletoe in his jauntily angled cap and a heavy coat over his ticket machine and leather money bag.

'Eddie,' called the inspector, 'this bus is late, you take it out as conductor, Jack will have to crew another bus when I find him.'

Eddie jumped on the bus, whistling. 'Right,' he said, 'let's go and get the engine started for some warmth here.'

He was about to ring the bell, when he saw the old man with the suitcase standing at the bus stop. 'Hoi,' he shouted, 'where you going?'

'Pontardawe,' was the reply.

'Pontardawe...well, this bus goes through there, hop on... here, give me your suitcase!' Out of that canteen, at exactly the right time, Eddie, the Angel of Neath Bus Station, had appeared. There was a busload, one over the permitted total, but rammed, jammed full of Christmas cheer all the way.

The Neath Market was always a must in my boyhood years on those shopping trips with my mother because of the cafe stalls in the back, where the speciality was faggots and peas followed by apple tart and custard. It was a ritual, in the same way that the Windsor Cafe was in Swansea, where the fish and chips came with bread and butter, and the tea was always served in teapots by waitresses dressed in black and white uniforms. My mother thought that added a touch of class to proceedings. Eating out was an indulgence for my mother because she was tied to the routines of housekeeping at home and, with four men in the house, it was heavy going.

My father and two of my mother's brothers, Illtyd and Thomas, were often on different shifts at work. Add me, at school, and meal times tended to be an evermoving conveyor belt rota. Cafe meals then, for my mother, were her particular pleasure, where the food was made for her; a break from cooking, which was always difficult because it was done on a coal fire (electric cookers were machines of the future in our house). I tended to like that pleasure of cafe visits too, except sometimes at the Windsor café on occasions, when we had to share a table. I hated that, especially when Mam would inevitably glance at what the other people were eating and say, 'I wish I'd ordered that now.'

On my historically more recent visit to the market, Napoleon marched into my mind. It was not so much the hemorrhoids question, though I'd love to have it verified as to whether it affected the outcome of Waterloo, one way or another. No, it was the news I'd picked up that suggested Napoleon had been in Neath and had stayed, far away from Josephine and the sophistication of Paris, in the Castle Hotel. In fact, there was talk of a touristy titbit displayed in the hotel that stated boldly: 'Napoleon slept here.'

I ventured to explore. I saw no framed declaration of the fact, but the rumour was strong and intoxicating. I was allowed to see the famed bed chamber and I was even allowed to lie on the duvet, just to give me a sense of being at one with history. Alongside the bed there was a small flight of portable steps to aid the intrepid climber. They were the original, I was assured; Napoleon had apparently used them, because the bed was tall and he was short.

So, a claim to fame for me was that I had slept in a bed used by Napoleon and, I hasten to boast, by Richard Burton and Elizabeth Taylor on one of their visits to

Pontrhydyfen. Sadly, further research diminished the tale somewhat, in that I found out that it was not Napoleon who had slept in the Castle Hotel, but Lord Nelson. Same incident, same period, same first letter in the Christian name, but different man. Still, Nelson was short, so he probably did use the steps. I cannot vouch for Richard Burton and Elizabeth Taylor, but I'm sure they would have had a go, just for the adventure and the sheer exciting hell of it. Certainly I clambered those steps.

To be fair, The Castle Hotel does have clear, bona fide claims to fame, as well as Nelson's one-night stand, of course. The Welsh Rugby Union was set up there when, in 1881, eleven clubs gathered in an upstairs room: Swansea, Pontypool, Newport, Merthyr, Llanelli, Bangor, Brecon, Llandovery, Lampeter and Llandeilo. Neath, oddly, was not listed, but, being that the grand meeting was in the town, it is assumed that representatives from Neath were in attendance, listed as being from the South Wales Football Club.

An earlier gathering of nine clubs had occurred in 1880 in the Tenby Hotel, Swansea, but, allegedly, no written evidence of the meeting survives and the accolade goes to Neath. The Castle Hotel management will allow you to visit the committee room on the first floor at which the clubs gathered for the the WRU's birth, and interesting photographs of past rugby heroes are dotted around the room.

In that room, the one character and player that always comes to my mind is Brian Thomas. Oxbridge graduate and three times a Cambridge Blue, metallurgist, philosopher, renowned rugby coach and, in his day, a rampaging second row lock forward. A warrior, and rough with it. He'd be the first to admit that if he did on a pavement what he did on the pitch, he'd get eighteen months for it.

I once met him at Deri Rugby Club, during a dinner at which we were both speaking. At one point in the evening I visited the gents comfort corner. In came Brian Thomas and stood, quietly, but with obvious presence, in the next trough to mine. After a moment, he spoke. 'You from Brynaman, are you? Best chips in the world come from Brynaman, you know...Brynaman and Brynmawr. It's all to do with the height above sea level and the atmospheric pressure on the chip fat.' Looking up at him, who was I to argue?

The Castle Hotel throws up another claim to historical 'goings on'. It was once reputed to be one of the most haunted buildings in Britain. At the time, if you were after spirits, you wouldn't be short changed in The Castle. There was an array of choice: a lady in black gliding down the staircase, a boy dressed in Edwardian clothes in the bar, a young girl floating quickly along the corridor, a poltergeist in one room (the number of the room was withheld), a chambermaid upstairs, a baying wolf in the cellar and a cavalier in the restaurant. You probably had to book early to get room there, you couldn't turn 'round for phantoms.

Of course, nowadays there is no special 'Ghost Convention' annually. Nothing as organised as that. The spectres haven't been on a rota for quite a while, when they were known to have manifested themselves as the moment took them. Disappointingly then, I'm told, not too many spectres have registered over the past years, but the spirits for sale in the safety of the bar really do make up for their absence, in quality and regularity. So do visit, the hotel has been wonderfully refurbished, and be enmeshed in the history; the visit of Nelson, if not Napoleon, Richard Burton and Elizabeth Taylor, the short steps as an aid in clambering to bed...that bed. Visit the convention room upstairs, keeping left on the staircase in case the lady in black has booked in, and remember the early rugby pioneers who set the Welsh Rugby Union loose amongst the nations of the world.

As for the spiritually in tune, be entranced by the past visitations and enriched and relaxed by the forty per cent proof spirits on offer at the bar's relaxing and comforting modern-day offerings. After which, sleep well. *Iechyd da.*

3. Llanwonno in Natal

Llanwonno

'They weren't singing, we were!' was the telephoned response to my piece of radio programme information in 2004 that the film *Zulu*, starring Stanley Baker and Michael Cain, was forty years old. My intrigue covered the quandary as to who was not singing, and why, and who exactly was singing and for what reason.

It was quickly made clear.

'When the Zulus were attacking the barricades at Rorke's Drift, in the film,' the man continued, 'and Ivor Emmanual started leading the men in a full pelt rendering of 'Men of Harlech', they were miming...we were singing.'

So, who were 'we'?

'The Imps,' he said, 'The Imperial Choir of Ferndale.'

It was true. We checked it out. The Imps had been asked to record the song on the car park of the Brynffynnon Hotel in Llanwonno, on the central moorland between Mountain Ash, Ynysybwl and Ferndale.

'And we had to record it a dozen times at least,' he continued, 'because as the boys sang they shuffled about a bit and the sound of the car park chippings was picked up by the microphones...and there's no chippings in Zululand.'

Now, Llanwonno is a lovely place, isolated in wondrous woodland, with only two buildings there: the fine-welcoming, thirst-quenching well that is the Brynffynnon, and St Gwynno's Church across the road. Add the repast to replenish the body and a sweeping treescape to sooth the soul and it's not a bad place to rest a while. Do take note of any chippings in the car park as well, for you can't get them in Zululand for love nor money, apparently. The next time you view *Zulu*, look closely to see if you can spot any of the Red Coats miming; it will add an extra dimension to your enjoyment.

So, to St Gwynno's Church. Just inside the gate of the churchyard, to the right, is the grave of Griffith Morgan of Nŷth Bran Farm, the Crow's Nest, where his father ran a sheep farm. Griffith's nickname was Guto and Guto Nŷth Bran was to enter Welsh legend as a runner, faster than a harassed hare, swifter than a swallow riding on a tail wind. His feats spread across The Valleys, his exploits no doubt embroidered on occasions, but he was, indeed, in the early eighteenth century, a man ahead of his time in sprinting and distance running. The Olympic team officials would have been seeking out Llanwonno and Guto to sign him up, with a supply of goose grease readily sponsored. One claim was that he slept in a dung heap to strengthen his legs.

Once, his mother sent him on an errand to Llantrisant or Aberdare and Guto asked her to put a kettle on the fire for a cup of tea on his return. He sprinted there and back before the kettle came to the boil. He didn't need a sheepdog to gather in a flock of sheep and he ran against all comers and horses for wagers. Race after race marked him up as victorious. Sian, his sweetheart, is said to have organised a race on Hirwaun Common against an unbeaten Englishman. He won easily, and claimed a prize of £400, big money in those days.

At the age of 30 he gave it all up, but at the age of 37 he was persuaded by Sian to come out of retirement to race against a 'new name on the block', a man named Prince, known as the Prince of Bedwas, over a distance of twelve miles from Newport to Bedwas. Hundreds of pounds were laid as bets and the prize money was 1000 guineas, a fortune. There was no public transport, so Guto walked to Newport to meet the challenge. In the race, Guto was laid back, shaking hands with well-wishers en-route. Then, remembering the huge prize money, he took off in earnest. Opposition supporters spread glass on the road, but to a leaping Guto they proved no bother at all. He caught and passed the insult-throwing Prince, breasting the tape as a wondrous victor. It is said that Sian,who was by now a kind of trainer and manager, was so excited that she ran up to Guto and, in unthinking enthusiasm, slapped him on the back, with cries of, 'Well done, Guto, well done.'

Not a good thing to do when a man is gasping for breath and his blood is pumping...you could hear the gasps of horror as far away as Caerffili as Guto crumpled and died in Sian's arms. It was 18th September 1737.

His body lies in Llanwonno churchyard and a gravestone recording how he died was placed there some years later, in 1866. There's a statue in his memory on the main street in Mountain Ash.

In his honour, races are held there every New Year's Eve, the Nôs Galan Races. They were inaugurated by Bernard Baldwin in 1958, the year the Commonwealth Games were held in Cardiff, for which Baldwin had acted as Press Officer. Hundreds take part; after a church service in St Gwynno's Church, a wreath is laid on Guto's grave and a mystery runner carries a lighted flare on a run to Mountain Ash, down in the Cynon Valley.

Now, you have to think, had Guto married and fathered

children, how many would have gone on to win gold medals in the Commonwealth and Olympic Games? Then again, no wagers are allowed in those games. There are no races around the track against horses, but officials would make sure that no glass is thrown in the lanes from spectators with vested interests.

Being that you are in the Cynon Valley, why not take in the setting for four more stories of fact and fancy?

In 1861, the first official National Eisteddfod was held in Aberdare. Forget about the first mentioned, in Cardigan Castle in 1176 A.D., the many unofficial ones held in taverns throughout Wales and the one held in the same year as the French Revolution, 1789. Aberdare gets the nod as the first official National Eisteddfod of the modern era.

It was planned to be held on the common land between Aberdare and Hirwaun, which is now Aberdare Park. The weather did not co-operate, however, and the marquee was damaged, so drastic alternative action was required.

Now, it is said that the storm was the result of religion in direct action. Allegedly, the chapel deacons throughout the valley did not view an eisteddfod as an acceptable festival for the pious, the pure, and those seeking enlightenment of the mind and a cleansing of the soul on the narrow road that skirted temptation in nifty side steps. Culture was one thing, but enjoyment, unleashed and unconfined, was another.

The story goes that an evening of prayer was set up to hinder or even waylay the eisteddfodic planning. The Christian cabal crossed non-conformist denominations and the effect of the combined prayer by deacons, some dedicated, some demented, in six-cylinder power, was awesome to behold. The storm built, the winds blew, the rains flowed in torrents and the tempest was too much for the tent. The marquee collapsed.

All was lost. The National Eisteddfod was doomed. But no, entrepreneurs of cultural competition were up to the task. 'Let's head for the market,' was the cry. So it came to pass that the first National Eisteddfod of the modern era was held in 1861, in Aberdare Market. Prof. Hywel Teifi Edwards, a few years ago, unveiled a blue plaque on the market wall to commemorate the event.

Head out of Commercial Street and on to Victoria Square and there it is: the statue of Griffith Rhys Jones, commonly known as Caradog; blacksmith, musician and conductor of the famous Côr Mawr of some 460 voices in the South Wales Coral Union, which twice won first prize at the Crystal Palace choral competitions in London in 1872 and 1873. Born in the Rose and Crown pub in Trecynon and buried in the town cemetery, he came from a talented family. His brother John was a tremendous musician and mathematician and ended up working for the Admiralty. He taught Griffith the violin, but Griffith was so short he had to rest the violin on the floor like a cello.

Caradog's statue is hugely impressive, standing there holding his baton to the sky. Sometimes, if the Saturday nights have been ribald in the town, the baton is sheltered from any rain by a neatly placed red and white traffic cone.

Did he leave an added mark on Welsh culture and character? That is the question. It is said that when the choir was in London, after the Crystal Palace successes, it was asked to sing for Queen Victoria. Afterwards, she was heard to say, 'Ah, Wales is truly the land of song.' Was that the first time the observation was made, the nomenclature bestowing upon us what is now a world accepted title? Quite possibly so, unless someone knows something different. After all, there is always someone, somewhere, who knows something about everything.

Along the road from Victoria Square, call in at two buildings, Aberdare Library and St John's Church. The Church goes back to Norman times, but behind the door there is a plaque that connects Aberdare to the Alamo, in San Antonio, Texas, and the eighteeth century, not the twelfth of the Norman era.

If you visit the Alamo, where the siege made famous by John Wayne as Davy Crocket in the film was enacted for real in 1836, you'll see flags of many nations. They represent the individuals who formed a kind of international brigade, making their stand for a future Texas against President General Antonio Lopez de Santa Anna and his Mexican army.

In the line of flags is the Welsh Red Dragon. When I first mentioned this on radio, two people contacted me, one stating that the Welsh representative was Lewis Johnson from Maesteg, another agreeing in part, stating that he was indeed Lewis Johnson, but he was from Neath. There is now a consensus that both were wrong. If Lewis Johnson was Welsh at all, he was, possibly, a second generation Welshman in America. But still the Red Dagon flies on the ancient ramparts of the Alamo at San Antonio de Bexar.

There was rumour of another Welshman who was

there, one John Rees of Merthyr Tydfil, an accomplished fifer. I'm not sure how he managed it, but the story goes that he was at the first skirmishes in 1835 and somehow got away and returned to Newport. Being of a rebellious and 'show me an insurrection and I'll be there' frame of mind, he later took part in the Chartist attack on the Westgate Hotel in Newport in 1839. There is a question, in fact, as to whether he fired the first shot, because he felt that the confrontation with the troops was rather too subdued for his liking and things were falling a bit flat.

The Welsh connection at the Alamo is definitely documented, however, by Major General Edward Edwards, who died there. It states so on the plaque behind the door at St John's Church. He had connections with Aberdare and Treherbert and was working for the British East India Company. He was commissioned, allegedly, to sell guns to the Mexicans, so, depending on how you look at things, with the Alamo having entered the nation's psyche thanks to the event and the famed film, Edward Edwards clearly died supporting 'the other side'. That's why, perhaps, his plaque is behind the door of St John's rather than on an imposing wall.

One hundred yards from St John's is Aberdare Library and another plaque recalling another conflict: the Spanish Civil War. Halfway up the stairs to the reading and research room, there are two points of interest. On one wall hangs a painting of *Kanchenjunga from Darjeeling* by Edward Lear, who wrote, amongst other things, *The Owl and the Pussy Cat*. He had been commissioned to paint it by the first Lord Aberdare in 1873 and it was given to the local council by a later Lord Aberdare in 1924. It was also given, at some point, to the Mountain Ash Urban District Council, where it was displayed for some years before being hung on the stairwell wall at Aberdare Library.

A knowledgeable visitor happened upon it and suggested that it might be genuine...and so it was. It was subsequently sold to the National Museum of Wales for £300,000 in 2003-2004. The painting now hanging halfway up the library stairs is a copy, but with a tale to tell.

So, to the plaque in that stairwell. It is a fine piece, with the names of all the Aberdare men who went to answer the call for members to join the International Brigade and fight General Franco and the fascists in Spain. On the list is Edwin Greening, a miner, teacher, local council member and a life-long communist. When I was a young buck teacher he was coming to the end of his teaching career, but we were members of the same Trade Union, the National Association of Schoolmasters, as was, now the NAS/UWT.

As was the tradition with teaching unions, we organised our national conferences at Easter time, in places like Harrogate, Torquay and Scarborough. One year, in the mid-1960s, an official had a flash of insightful inspiration. 'Hey,' he ventured, 'with these packaged holiday deals to Spain and Majorca, we can organise our five-day conferences there. It will be quids cheaper.' His suggestion was duly minuted and sent off to National Headquarters. Officials there thought it was a marvellous idea. There was hot-foot planning and the sun and surf beckoned alongside the conference itinerary and educational list of motions for the good of pupils, teachers and schools.

Then came Edwin's note, a note that put a damper and a brake on proceedings.

'I can't go there,' he said, 'I fought against Franco in the Spanish Civil War. Franco's still alive, so I'm on his list, I must be. The list to be shot.'

We went to Harrogate instead.

4. Penderyn Spirits

Penderyn

You'll feel it if you sit in the corner seat. That's what's believed anyway. It's the seat with a high back, near the fire, but, ignoring the wood fire flames, the creeping cold will set out to get you. That's where the soldier sits, in the far corner of the pub, the Red Lion.

It was during the Napoleonic War, early nineteenth century, that he came. Looking for canon fodder, the locals said, seeking out young bucks of the parish and, if willing, more mature stags as well to take the King's shilling. The army ranks needed swelling, so the trawl was on. The soldier sat, drinking, being sociable, stretched back in the chair, his uniform red but untidy, scruffy, for the soldiers, in many cases, had to buy their own uniform, so an unkempt one was cheaper. He was on a mission, recruitment, and there were quite a few tempting coins about his person.

It was an attraction for those seeking new experiences, a taste of something beyond the rural expanse and large, hard-pressed country families, or the trials of life around Merthyr Tydfil facing the furnaces of the spreading iron works and the coming of the coal. Accepting the offer gave a chance of life beyond the beyond for eyes seeking far horizons. Danger was firmly kept in the pocket of the colourful coat called 'adventure'.

Those more wary of being tricked into commitment to a military life were careful, as long as they were sober. Many of the drinking jars had glass bottoms, so that in lifting it to your mouth you could check whether a shilling had been quietly dropped into it. It was thought that if you drank your fill, down to where the shilling lay, then it could be said that you were definitely signed up, in front of witnesses. It was commitment to the ranks.

The soldier was based at the pub for some time. Then, one day, he'd gone, disappeared; his work done, perhaps, or was there more to it? Some months later, the soldier's red coat, unkempt as it was, had an airing...on the back of the inn-keeper. Rumours travel miles before truth can get its boots on, whether they are on the road or in someone's imagination. Had the inn-keeper 'done him in'? Added intriguing chapters were to bubble the broth for some time. Tales of him being tied to a chair, beaten so that he'd reveal where he kept all those shillings. The inn-keeper could not be questioned too keenly, for he was also the local constable.

What of the scene, though? What of the pub, the village, the area, the wintry mist covered expanse of moorland that leads towards the upper Taff Valley and beyond the slopes of Pen y Fan, down to Brecon and the farmlands of the Usk river?

Penderyn is an ancient place. The Red Lion stands on the hilltop, opposite St Cynog's Church. The church tower was constructed as a secure holding place for Norman soldiers, at the side of a track that ran from Neath to Brecon. It was a place of wildness, so security for the traveller was required. The men who built the tower were housed in a building that formed the foundations, in part, of the present-day pub. So, the scene takes us back to around 1120 A.D.

St Cynog's Church has a cemetery that has, so it is said, over 10,000 graves. One of the gravestones has a relative of Anne Boleyn named as the occupant. Allegedly, the

Boleyn family had dispersed far and wide after the shame and scandal suffered following Anne's execution. Perhaps they felt that Penderyn was a safe arm's length away from Henry VIII's reach. It has also been suggested that, for various reasons, families within coffin carrying distance of St Cynog's Church felt the effort worthwhile, due to a certain kudos being attached to being buried there. The graveyard is circular, giving hints that the ground was sacred from a period before the Romans came. One wonders whether there was an early booking scheme for a plot, bearing in mind the numbers within the sacred circle.

If you travel down the hill from the church and cross the main road, the Cwm Cadlan Road takes you along a moorland expanse that hides in its undergrowth, sometimes not too successfully, the foundations of Bronze Age houses and evidence of pre-Roman activity. They are clearly seen if you know where to look. Some of the locals, deep-rooted residents, probably go back, in bloodline, to the Bronze Age and beyond. We are all, in lineage, from somewhere else. We are all early immigrants. Genealogy is now hugely popular and many of us seek out the answer to 'Who do you think you are?' There is a new service for avid seekers. DNA Cymru can take you back 15,000 years. It is simply done; you spit into a test tube, jump on the Tardis and away you go.

In my case, my mother's family came from the Basque Country of Spain and France, travelling with the Beaker folk and early farmers. My father's far-off roots are more of a shaker. My spit took me back to the homeland, somewhere between northern Iraq, Turkey and Georgia.

I try and keep a low profile about the Georgia connection because, coming down through the strata of generations, one of my great-uncles could have been Joseph Stalin.

The one great fillip about Georgia is that I once spoke to a businessman from Bridgend who had done a lot of work in that neck of the woods. Aside from being mugged at a roadblock, manned by a soldier who demanded money because he hadn't been paid, plus a side tip for his sergeant in the road-side shed, he came across a valley that seemed a gateway to Shangri-La. In that valley, people seemed to live to a great age. He came across a male voice choir of centurions; in fact, the youngest chorister, a top note tenor, was 100. The reason, apparently, was the diet, the pace of life and a secret yoghurt. If I find the place, I'll be importing that stuff by the tankerful!

Back from the Greater Caucasus mountain range then, to the Brecon Beacons and Penderyn. One has to admit, whatever its joys, any possible male voice choir members locally wouldn't be expected to reach the century mark and the local product is not yoghurt but rather known as 'the water of life'. More on that shortly.

The remains of the original church at Penderyn can be seen to the right of the tower, merely as a mound of earth, if you look from the Red Lion car park. When the sun has just set and the sky is clear, the church and gravestones stand like eerie, atmospheric sentinels against the sky. The present building dates from the seventeenth century. Unfortunately, the church recently closed, clearly lacking posteriors on pews.

The road between St Cynog and the Red Lion developed,

from an early track into an important drovers' road. That was the commercial animal route from Neath to Brecon via Cwm Cadlan, and it was joined at the pub by a side road leading back to the Cynon Valley and, over the ridge, to the Rhondda.

For those with ancient receptors in their body, there is also a suggestion that the place harbours a confluence of pre-historic ley lines. The tribes of long-past eons, way back, were well into ley lines apparently. They were well plugged in to mother earth, with all its benefits and deficits.

There can be positive and negative ley lines, so I'm told. Which ones mark out the grid in Penderyn, I wonder? Locals might be able to give us a clue if you chat them up.

There has been a pub on the Red Lion site for hundreds of years. In the very early days it was called Tafarn Uchaf, the Upper Tavern. It was a Welsh longhouse design. It stayed true to its roots and design until recently, when the old, empty animal section was transformed into a restaurant and, glory be, new indoor toilets were installed. Prior to those developments, the men's toilet was the stuff of legend; it was open air...and up the road. Visiting it on a fresh February night could severely affect a man's personality, but it had a kind of democracy about it, for the cold, bracing, hilltop air ensured that out there in the elements all men were rendered equal.

Down the slope, back to the northern part of the village, you'll find the Lamb Inn. It stands across the road from where the Cwm Cadlan Road joins the main road. It is a pub of history, with a more recent story that has merited a Blue Plaque on its wall.

During the insurrection in Merthyr Tydfil many of the demonstrators fled, one headed in the Penderyn direction. His friend was Dick Penderyn, whose hanging has entered the annals of infamy in Welsh history. The village of Penderyn refugee was Lewis yr Heliwr, Lewis the Hunter. He was finally caught on the Foel Hill that rises up behind the Lamb, the church and the Red Lion, kept in the Lamb cellar overnight and then taken to Cardiff. He escaped hanging but was transported to Australia.

Incidentally, the spot on which Dick Penderyn was hanged is where Church Street and Quay Street meet High Street, Cardiff, at the top end of St Mary Street. Dic was taken from Cardiff Prison to meet his fate, and the prison in those days was where Cardiff indoor market now stands.

Down the main road, past the limestone quarries towards Hirwaun, you step on several other historical trails. One leads to the site of the old Hirwaun Ironworks, leased by members of a famous Heads of the Valleys industrial heritage family, the Crawshays. Although originally from Yorkshire, they became synonymous with the Industrial Revolution and the production of iron in Merthyr Tydfil and its hinterland. Wlliam Crawshay II sent his son Henry as manager of the Hirwaun works and he became involved with a young girl from Penderyn named Eliza Harris, who was employed there. His father's intervention proved fruitless and Eliza and Henry were married. Their son, also named Henry, was christened at Penderyn Church. Unfortunately, young Henry died, but the couple went on to have twin daughters who were christened at Nebo Chapel, Hirwaun. Nebo Chapel was recently the subject of a televised restoration project, undertaken by a young couple who bought it for a song, or, more appropriately, a hymn.

So, back to the soldier's tale. Where did he go? Did he manage to spend the King's shillings and gather recruits before departing? How was it that the soldier's uniform was seen being worn by the innkeeper? The questions lengthened when an incident happened at the rear of the pub some years after his disappearance. A section of the garden wall collapsed and, it was rumoured, human remains were found there. Investigations did not get far. As the local constable, the innkeeper was in a telling position to keep a heavy foot on vexing queries. Come to think of it, there is still a section of the back garden wall that is wider than the rest, so one is left wondering.

The really sobering visitation, however, occurred relatively recently. It was a lady from the Low Countries. It was mid-afternoon when a group from the Netherlands entered the pub. The lady had a wild look about her. Eyes staring, seeking, her hair standing almost on end, frizzed as if by a fright. 'What is the power and the odd vibes I feel from the churchyard?' she questioned loudly. Whether it was the ley line power she felt or perhaps her sensors were a little off beam, picking up something that was not in the pub but on the other side of the road.

Her male companion quietened her down and led her to a chair...the corner chair with the high back. He had not been at the bar ordering drinks for more than two minutes when she came charging up to him. 'Who is that man in the red coat sitting in the corner with blood on his face, manacled to the chair?' She was describing the soldier from centuries before.

Apparently, the lady was in a highly-charged and sensitive state when she came to Penderyn. Her husband had died suddenly and her son had been killed in a car crash shortly afterwards. She was entirely open to dark vibes floating in the breezes about the churchyard, the Red Lion and the hilltop air. Her visit and experience was an unnerving event, and is still talked about.

In modern-day Penderyn spirits still abound, but they are more aligned with the 'water of life' than any dredge of despair: the Welsh whisky distillery opened there at the kick off of this century. Gin, vodka and the cream liqueur of the ancients, Merlyn, all from the vats, casks and bottles, but the greatest of these is Penderyn whisky itself. The vision of possibility came from a group of men who met in the Glan Cynon pub, in Hirwaun. One was Alun Evans, at one time the youngest landlord in the Valley at just nineteen years of age. He sadly passed on recently, but his gravestone has the proud and unique golden stripe on it that is the Penderyn emblem: *Aur Cymru*, Welsh Gold... and so it is.

There is talk that the Welsh invented whisky, not the Irish, nor the Scots, but were we ever pushy as entrepreneurs? No. I think that was neutered by our patron saint, St David. He was a teacher, a preacher, a frugal, pious man of no excesses, lest he be found wanton. That tends to water down hot blood, or any ambition that's a step away from the straight and narrow, don't you think?

5. The Rhigos Ridge

Treherbert Road

Time is an interlinked trinity. Foresight, insight and hindsight. How can you ever have the foresight of knowing where you are going, without having the insight of assessing where you are, and appreciating the hindsight of what has moulded you as a person, in being, in memory and in self and in bringing you to where you are? Past events and people were the sculptors that brought you here and honed your potential and interest. Those sculptors are never on short time or a three-day week. They continue their work, anytime, anyplace.

'If you turn and face east near the burger and ice cream van, the next highest land you come to is in the Urals of Russia!' That's what I was told, with authority, in a pub in Glynneath. It could be so, for this is an area of uncertain truths and elastic facts.

Where is the strategic van in question? Well, it's in the lay-by that faces north on the Rhigos ridge, alongside the road from Hirwaun to Treherbert. Speaking geographically, the ridge is the high escarpment that marks the northern edge of the South Wales Coalfield and the lay-by has fine, dramatic views looking down on the site of Tower Colliery on Hirwaun Common, as well as Llyn Fawr. Once a glacial lake sheltered by Graig y Llyn, but was enlarged at the beginning of the twentieth century to provide a reservoir for urban water supply, easing the thirst of the expanding valleys population. Raise your eyes and in the far distance you can clearly see the highest mount in south Wales: Pen y Fan in the Brecon Beacons.

When Llyn Fawr was excavated, a hoard of Bronze Age artifacts, weapons and utensils, including an impressive cauldron for cooking, were discovered in the mud and lake bottom strata. They are now in the National Museum of Wales, Cathays, Cardiff. The story goes that they seemed to have been hurriedly dumped there by a local tribe who had to leave at a pace, probably because of unwelcome visitors from a patch further afield.

The spot has a special meaning and is a magnet for me. Just down the road, there is a small car park from which you can view the upper reaches of the Rhondda Fawr, to Treherbert, Blaenrhondda and the flat-topped ridge that looks like it's been borrowed from a Western film.

Once a year, between Christmas and the New Year, I go to the car park, looking west to a far-off waterfall and one solitary, lonely, moorland conifer tree. There, with a bottle of whisky, two tumblers and a few droplets of water, I raise a glass to a great friend of mine whose ashes are scattered there on the high moorland between the Rhondda and Cynon Valleys; one the valley of his birth, the other the valley of his passing. He was a renowned minister, preacher, poet and writer, winning two National Eisteddfod crowns, and began to write in English in his later years. He wrote scripts for Granada Television, including *Coronation Street*, and swore blind to me that he was the one who came up with the title for the soap opera, the original name being 'Florizel Street'.

He was a fully paid-up bon vivant and bon viveur, even from his modest terraced HQ in Llewelyn Street, Trecynon. He knew Richard Burton and Elizabeth Taylor and gloried with joy in people and name-dropping. I first met him after he'd had a stroke, but in the twenty years that followed that mere comma on his excesses, I called in on him weekly to chat and to sup the 'water of life'. His bed-study was behind the kitchen on the ground floor and he had two bottles under his bed, one for his natural needs, the other being Famous Grouse, his tipple. I supplied the nectar and on one occasion when I tried a new brand, cheaper and 'on offer', he gently said, 'Roy, men of station and standard like us two should not deem to lower ourselves to the level of this hooch.'

He was also the man who taught me understanding and Christian flexibility in my dealings with others.

'Roy, as a minister of religion, I confess to having trouble with two of the Ten Commandments, but, to be fair, these days a mark of eight out of ten is an A* in most exams. Remember, too, be charitable; don't push a man too far. Stretch the elastic too far and the snap back could catch you out regally. I recall being in the pulpit one Sunday night, the *hwyl*, the fire, the brimstone and charismatic power being upon me. In a moment when the surge went over the cliff, I shouted, "Confess, confess your sins. You, Idwal Davies in pew three, think back in purity, have you ever stepped off the righteous path, succumbed and slept with another woman beyond your household, your wife?" The reply, Roy, hit me like a whiplash, and I deserved it. "No, I have not slept with another woman...but I may have dozed off once or twice!"' It certainly caused a few fuses to falter in his future sermons, he assured me of that.

That is the beauty of these places that hold stories of old and tales of the ancients. Added personal glimpses fly back to colour each spot with murals from your own memories.

Tower Colliery, now closed, is still the symbol of defiance from when the miners bought the mine as government policy declared the death knell for the coal industry elsewhere. Oddly, Hirwaun Common is the moorland on which, so it is claimed, the first red flag of insurrection was flown. The Russian Revolution was a Johnny-come-lately in terms of red flags flying. During the years 1828-1831, trouble was brewing in the Heads of the Valleys. The Merthyr Rising, the most significant people's protest since Owain Glyndŵr went walkabout in Wales, had been preceded by a rally at Hirwaun organised by Thomas Llewelyn, a coal miner. A major depression had come like a cloud to the industrial area, the value of iron fell and men were paid in truck tokens, coins or notes that could only be spent in company shops, where the prices were inflated and the quality of goods questionable.

It was in May 1829 that Thomas Llewelyn's rally gathered on Hirwaun Common and some people there wanted more radical reform. A white scarf was dipped in the blood of a calf, raised high on a pole and became the first red flag flown anywhere as a left-wing symbol. The slogan was 'Bara neu gwaed', 'Bread or blood'.

On the matter of the Merthyr Rising, I once made a mistake when interviewing the radical socialist historian Prof. Gwyn Alf Williams as we walked through Merthyr Tydfil. I asked him about the Merthyr *Riot*. 'Now listen to me, Roy,' he responded, 'there was never a riot in Merthyr... mind you, there was a bloody good rising!'

Incidentally, the Tower Colliery got its name from a

tower built nearby in 1847. It was put up by the ironmasters of the Crawshay family in defence against any future rebellion. The ruins of the tower lie unseen now, in the undergrowth of the common.

Back to that ice cream lay-by, and if you stretch, you can make out the low moorland between Pontneddfechan, Pontneathvaughan in English, and Ystradfellte. On the moorland beyond Ystradfellte, the Roman road, Sarn Helen, heads you towards the Senni Valley. Alongside the road there are two standing stones, Maen Llia and Maen Madoc, and on Maen Madoc there was the Latin inscription, now faded: 'Dervacus Filius Justi Ic Jacit' – 'Dervacus, son of Justus, lies here'.

Dervacus was a a sixth-century Roman name, some 200 years after the Romans were recalled to defend the Roman Empire from the eastern hordes. The Romans left but the names remained, possibly. Then again, the stone could have been erected in Bronze Age times, thus making the inscription more perplexing. It appears that it was moved at least once, further from Sarn Helen, possibly after falling over. So if Dervacus was buried there, then the stone does not mark his exact resting place.

The sweep from Pontneddfechan to Ystradefellte is known as waterfall country, with spectacular waterfalls on the rivers Mellte, Hepste and Nedd Fechan, blessed as it is with beautiful scenery, dramatic gorges and numerous caves for the more adventurous visitor. This is also limestone country, a rock with which I've had a lifelong calling and love affair. I was born below the Black Mountain of Carmarthenshire, on the western edge of the

Brecon Beacons, but it is a myth-laden high moorland that is less showy and chesty than the Beacons. The limestone link extends to Pontneddfechan, where I became a village headmaster for the first time, as well as Llangattock, near Crickhowell, the village where I was also the headteacher, and Penderyn, where my son and daughter-in-law live, just five miles from our own home near Aberdare. Limestone seems to have drawn me in like a magnet.

At the far end of the village of of Pontneddfechan, history throws up three other tales to set the body wandering and the mind wondering. Two offer truth, the other is fanciful, well, fanciful but somehow reassuring.

Silica lies with limestone in a kind of hostel arrangement with adjoining beds of strata. It was the home of a commodity that became international: the Dinas brick, named after Dinas Rock, a limestone promontory nearby. Although production in the village has long gone the brick is still available worldwide, hanging on to its name, notably in China and in Russia. The bricks, with their special silica properties, were destined for use in industrial furnaces and so significant were the bricks from this area during the Industrial Revolution that the word *dinas* entered into other languages, especially Russian, to mean any refractory brick at all.

Dinas Rock is sometimes incorrectly named Craig y Ddinas in Welsh. No need for mutation apparently, because *dinas* means 'fortress' or 'city', deriving its name from an Iron Age earthworks on its summit, so Craig Dinas is the correct translation. No doubt there will be debate and disagreements about that.

Along the Mellte River was situated the Glynneath Gunpowder Works, destined eventually to merge with the Nobel's Explosives Co, the Nobel of Nobel Prizes fame, of course. Each constituent building was placed 'round a river bend from another building, so that if there was an accidental explosion in one sector it did nor trigger a chain reaction. The remains of each building can still be seen today if you take a walk past the Pontneddfechan village hall, near Dinas Rock car park, and carry on along the high banks of the River Hepste.

All these historical highlights: Dinas Rock, which gave the word *Dinas* to the brick world, the Gunpowder Works, Maen Llia, Maen Madoc, Sarn Helen, Graig y Llyn above Rhigos and Tower Colliery are all within the short, leisurely flight of a disorientated crow who was bereft of a 'as the crow flies' straight line compass bearing. All can be seen or pinpointed from that ice cream van lay-by viewpoint on the Rhigos ridge. But, but, there is one more ingredient to the *cawl* of possibilities, and for it we go back to Dinas Rock, where myths and fables take over the mind.

It is said, you see, that around the base of Dinas Rock, there are a few short caves. Some are accessible, including Ogof Pont Sychryd, Ogof Bwa Maen, or the less lyrically and more earthily-named Will's Hole. There is one other, lost in antiquity but there for the exploring if needs must.

It is said that if Wales is ever seriously threatened, then an expedition should be quickly set up to seek out the hidden chamber. Fate and fancy will lead you to the entrance. Once found, clear the undergrowth and you will come across a bell hanging from the roof of the cave entrance. You are to ring the heavy bell, and at the end of its pealing you will hear a frenzied rustling and clambering from deep within the limestone tunnel. Do quickly step aside, lest you get run over, for out of the recesses will surge a phalanx of mounted cavalry. King Arthur and the boys, his Knights of the Round Table, will thunder into the open air, instinctively knowing where the danger lies and in a cloud of dust and a cry of 'High ho', plus whatever the name of their particular mount is, they will scatter in all directions, delving into a daring do and, glory be, saving us all. I often took a troop of schoolchildren down to Dinas Rock on a summer's day seeking out the cave, but to no avail. Rest assured though, be content and secure, I have a fair idea where it is, and carrying a powerful magnet I am confident I'll be drawn to the bell.

As for that lay-by, looking north across all I've reviewed, the one question still remains. On the latitude that the burger and ice cream van stands, if you turn east, is it true that the highest land you come to next is in the Ural Mountains of Russia? Check an atlas. I have, and there appears to be just one irritating range of hills in the way, but it could be so, it could be so...from Graig y Llyn to Gremyachinsk, unhindered.

6. Love in Llangynwyd

Llynfi Valley

'The answer is yes, of course it's yes, but think about it now, do you want to buy me a ring or a second-hand lorry?' That was the question that totally threw him on that balmy evening in June when betrothal was on the breeze. Love, lust and longing are powerful ingredients in the *cawl* or broth of yearning and pining. Add coveting to the mix and it becomes a spicy concoction indeed. Sometimes the attraction is so strong that obstacles are cast aside, however high and daunting, but on other occasions the path is riddled with fatal fault lines.

Success fell upon one unlikely couple in Wales. For the sake of discretion I'll call them Suzanne and Moelwyn. Suzanne showed unstinting determination in weaving a path to the altar. Her would-be suitor, Moelwyn, was the one who first showed an avid interest in bringing an attachment to fruition, but, in truth, he seemed to be whistling in the wind, for she was an 'uptown girl'. A maid of good stock, select breeding, several rungs up the ladder of social standing and several houses up the road from Moelwyn. She was definitely on the sunny side of town. He wasn't exactly from the other side of the tracks, as they say, just a touch too near the railway line, that's all. His home was solid and loving, which did give him an inner strength, security, and a feeling of being unique, to his mam anyway, having a right to be and with a contribution to make. All callow youths need that inner self-worth, but without being showy about it.

There was something about Moelwyn that Suzanne had first picked up in floating vibes during their time together in primary school. An academic he was not, long multiplication sums and the traps of comprehension exercises remaining foggy mysteries for him each unfolding term, but in young good looks and pleasing personality he more than held his own, even if the legs of his short trousers ended not too far from the top of his long socks. He was popular with the teacher and his classmates. In truth, he'd always liked Suzanne and as puberty began to pulse, the liking had gone up a couple of notches. For her, his performance as a hooker in the secondary school team had brought quiet, private smiles to her face as well, and had reinforced her feelings and interest. By the time their teenage years had moved into their twenties and she was back from college, he had picked up the signals and decided that he would throw his cap into the ring and go fishing on the sunny side of town, for there was nothing to lose, if a chance ever came up. She could only say no. Her parents had ambitions and aspirations for her though, and they threatened to be a mighty stumbling block.

She had noticed his roving eye coming to rest at sight of her many times, even as she just walked to the post office and, reacting to her own warming of the blood, she glanced back many times in encouragement. Moelwyn was irritatingly slow in her mind, so a telling move was required.

It was at the fairground she landed him, first near the dodgems, then the swings, and finally in the tent entitled 'Exotic Scenes from History' – only those over eighteen allowed in. Once inside, the exotic quickly became apparent. When the curtain opened, the first tableau was 'Boudicca on her chariot'. Through the gauze curtain it was clear that Boudicca's only protective armour for battle was a helmet and a spear. She wore nothing else. The second scene was 'Cleopatra on the banks of the Nile'. Her veil was held by a hand maiden and Cleopatra held clumps of reeds in strategic places. The third, 'Hiawatha', was a vision in Native American boots and a feathered headband. Apparently, as long as the models did not move, aping the rules in The Windmill Theatre, London, all was well and the Carmarthenshire constabulary felt no discomfort at all.

On retreat from the tent, Moelwyn finally made his move, using, so it is said, the killer courting line: 'Do you fancy some candy floss?' Her answering smile spoke paragraphs. She would have preferred a toffee apple, but who cared? The relationship was on a roll.

Over the following months, the courtship turned to coveting for Moelwyn and Suzanne was ahead of him in thought and deed. Her parents were less than keen, heading towards the absolutely livid in reaction. To no avail, for in the soft grass of the old Gorsedd Circle that sultry summer night, talk of an engagement was in the scented air.

To his question of commitment, it was then that she surprised him.

'The answer is yes, of course it's yes, but think about it now, do you want to buy me a ring or a second-hand lorry? He spluttered 'ring' but she countered, 'No, no, let's make it a lorry.'

There was definitely something in Moelwyn that she was determined to reach and her instinct was to prove oh so right.

That one second hand lorry has grown by now, over the years, to a fleet of lorries. Suzanne does the books, she deals with the letters, invoices, orders and bureaucracy, but Moelwyn has the gift. He has the talent for front-line, face to face business and negotiation. He is popular, affable. People feel safe with him. He is a success. Will their son or daughter go into the business? Who knows? Life on the sunny uptown side is good. The vision of the horizon for the next generation will be tempered by their own story, for that is the way of things.

Relationships are towards the top of the division in life's priorities. If relationships are right, personal or professional, then no steep hill on your path or caverns in your road can hinder you.

Love, lust and longing proved a potent mix in that relatively modern-day tale. It has not always been so when the social divide has come into play. As was the case of another century, another story, where the fault lines proved fatal, the barriers too high; but the moving, romantic legend has strayed into the soul of the nation, in song and fable. The song is the poignant 'Bugeilio'r Gwenith Gwyn' – 'Watching the White Wheat'. The fable is the famed 'Maid of Cefn Ydfa'.

The saga unfolded in Llangynwyd, Top Llan to be precise, the higher hamlet of the two Llangynwyds, just south of Maesteg on the main road to Bridgend. The Llynfi Valley has many tales from within its boundaries. Before coal became a magnet for developers, the iron works of Cambrian Llynfi attracted investment from people like William Wordsworth, the poet, and Sir Felix Booth, the gin distiller. The Maesteg town hall is a fine, Grade II listed building adorned in its main hall by wonderful murals, paintings by Christopher Williams, a local boy, who was described by Lloyd George as one of the greatest Welsh artists. Indeed, his is a story meriting its own chapter. His mother died a fortnight after his birth and he was christened on her coffin. Brought up, lovingly, by a wet nurse and her collier husband in Nantyfyllon, he was taken away from that poor but comfortable home and the woman he called Mam by his father, to live above the family grocery store. His dad held ambitions for his son to be a doctor, but a fortunate visit to Liverpool's Walker Gallery provided telling inspiration and a guiding vision that led him to art. He was a man of the people and, on his death, the flags were flown at half mast on Maesteg Town Hall.

Music also has a deep, everlasting tradition in Maesteg, in that several noted choirs are based in the town. In fact, the Welsh national anthem, 'Hen Wlad Fy Nhadau' – 'Land of my Fathers', under its original melody name, 'Glan Rhondda', was first performed in Maesteg, in the vestry of Capel Tabor, which is now Maesteg Working Men's Club.

So many stories to discover along the Llynfi, but it is Llangynwyd, Top Llan specifically, that holds the loving saga of The Maid of Cefn Ydfa. The village is historic on several levels, taking in the ancients and stepping down through the centuries. There are the tell-tale markings and mounds of the Iron Age fort, the limited ruins of a Norman Age castle and the impressive church of St Cynwyd, with its tightly-packed and surprisingly extensive cemetery, regarded as possibly the largest private cemetery in Europe.

Llangynwyd is also the only place in Wales that still celebrates the New Year, or *Calennig* of Mari Lwyd fame, where a horse's skull, draped in a white cloth with a supporting stick, is marched around the village. Stopping at each household, the men carrying the Mari Lwyd sing a few verses in poetic metre and a resident must respond in the same way. If they cannot, the group have to be invited inside for a drink. They are usually invited in anyway, regardless of whether the householder could respond poetically.

For the traveller or visitor to Top Llan seeking a refreshing oasis, or any of the boys carrying the Mari Lwyd who found that the welcome well was rather dry in a few of the houses, there are two pubs. The magnificent thatched Old House dates back to 1147 A.D. and the Corner House, which, originally, was three cottages, throws in a couple of ghosts as added attractions and dates back to 1755 A.D. Wil Hopcyn, thatcher, tiler, plasterer and poet, was said to have lived in the Corner House for a while. He was one of the doomed lovers in the poignant romance that has entered Welsh folklore, the other being Ann Thomas, the famed Maid of Cefn Ydfa.

Cefn Ydfa was an impressive residence in the Llynfi Valley. Ann's mother, Catherine, was sister to Rees Price, the father of Richard Price, philosopher, eccentric and romantic; he of 'first ever public cremation' fame, when he cremated his son, named Jesus Christ, in Llantrisant.

Ann's father died when she was young and the tale unfolds that she, as heiress, was placed in the wardship of Anthony Maddocks, a lawyer from Cwmrisga. Maddocks decided that Ann should marry his son, also called Anthony; Ann, however, had fallen in love with Wil Hopcyn, who had done some maintenance work at Cefn Ydfa. The attraction was mutual, but, when this was discovered, Ann was forbidden to see Wil. But often love will find a way and the couple continued to have a secret tryst, exchanging love letters with the aid of one of her maidservants and which were hidden in the hollow of an oak tree on the Cefn Ydfa estate.

Whether they were all successfully delivered, no one knows, but the arrangement was quickly found out; her mother confiscated all her quills, paper and other possible writing material. Legend has it that Ann took to writing on leaves plucked from the tree outside her bedroom, the ink being her own blood.

Pressure from the family mounted and, sadly, Ann succumbed and agreed to marry Anthony. It is said that on seeing Ann and her mother buying wedding paraphernalia in Bridgend Market, Wil was overcome by grief and left the area to take his craftsmanship to Bristol.

In the marriage, Ann pined so desperately for Wil that she became ill, physically and mentally, and on her death bed she cried out for Wil Hopkyn. He was sent for and, tragically, she died in his arms.

Ann, being from a noted family, was buried within St Cynwyd's church. Wil's passing was some years later and he was buried, naturally, outside the church. Some say he died from natural causes, others that it was after falling off a ladder in Llangynwyd. Now, romantics relate that

Wil's grave is so close to the church wall that his feet and Ann's feet are, in fact, almost touching. If this is the case, then either Wil's legs were over seven metres long or his gravestone has been moved, for it is clearly seen today leaning against a yew tree, some distance away from the church wall.

A heart-touching romantic tale? Many regard it as such, but others of a more pragmatic view throw a few sobering ingredients into the cauldron. Was Anthony such a bad choice as a husband in view of the sense of unifying two noted families? What of Wil? Was he the true besotted poet or had it struck him that Ann was a pretty good catch for a labouring man? Some have even suggested that he was, in truth, a braggart and a drunk.

So, what is the true story? Bearing in mind the evocative words and lilting melody of 'Bugeilio'r Gwenith Gwyn', and the fact that Wil, allegedly, wrote or co-wrote the words, if you have a drop of Celtic blood in your veins you can't go for the pragmatic, lawyer's view. You must lean towards pulsating and yearning love. You must feel for his loss when Ann married, in possibly his own words in the song:

'...I fondly watched the blooming wheat,
While others reap the treasure'

7. Senghenydd

Aber Valley

'What if? What if?' Short question, big ponder, useless exercise. How many times have we dwelt on events, on the small personal scale or on the vast repercussion level, just to wonder if little things or developments could have made a big different. How would it all have turned out? We all wonder at those lip-biting frustrations, but there's no point losing sleep over them. Fate has rolled the dice.

That question 'What if?' dwells on the past, something you cannot do anything about, but an often-used defensive statement of the present, promising so much for a better future, tends to be just as neutered in effect: 'Lessons will be learnt!'

How many times have you heard it as a shield against accusations of failure or inadequacy and how effective was it, really? Be honest now.

Both the question 'What if?' and the statement 'Lessons will be learnt!' are writ large in the history of Senghenydd. It is a village that has drawn me in to its being, its story, its soul, on three notable occasions.

The first was during college days, when Senghenydd Rugby Club were going through a lean period and the committee had asked a locally-born student to act as a missionary (or was he a mercenary?) to seek out spare players that the college team was not using. I was very much a spare part on the rugby front in the college. It was a Spartan wing of an establishment, with most of the boys training to be PE teachers, so the place was awash with warriors in green tracksuits with a permanent whiff of 'winter green or liniment' on every vibrant sinew. My subject was geography, so getting into the college rugby team was a no-hoper. I'd only get into the third team if there was a plague of gastroenteritus in the corridors and the teams were short of players.

So, I was invited to help Senghenydd. I confess to accepting expenses for my services, 'boot money', which was taboo in those days. If you were caught accepting money you were classed in the tainted category, along with darts and snooker players; the 'fee' was ten shillings. The game went reasonably well, but after my second run-out the following week the ten shillings came with a plea, a strong hint in fact, that if I could join and play for their main rivals then I would really be of help to them.

Fate is what happens to you, they say, and destiny is what you do with what happens to you. Fate and destiny fused some years later when I became a teacher at the local junior school, the old Senghenydd Primary School on the hill. My relationship with the village, without me realising it, was cementing at a deeper level. It was drawing me in for a second time. It was, in many ways, a familiar place to me, very valley, as they say. It had a square with a war memorial, places of worship, streets of terraced houses and large hostelries, built in the klondike years. One was intriguingly named 'The Ukrainian Club of Kiev'. Apparently, when first built it was the Universal Club. I was to work happily in the community for some years, under the headteacher and local historian Dai Parry.

Senghenydd, of course, has entered into the very fabric of industrial history in Wales. It has the deeply sad and poignantly dramatic distinction of having been ripped asunder by the largest coal mining disaster in British history. The story of what happened encloses the vagaries of men, their decisions, their inaction, their complacency and their arrogance.

Yet, the village has to be placed in context. Its story begins centuries before King Coal came on his state visit. It goes back to its earliest inhabitants, the tribes of the Bronze Age, who settled on Eglwysilian Common.

Fast-forward to the years following the Norman invasion and the local boy, the self entitled lord of Senghenydd, Ifor Bach, or Ivor the Short, was putting himself about. His full name was Ifor ap Meurig and he was to become a permanent carbuncle on the backsides of the Normans at Cardiff and Caerffili.

The old Welsh Kingdom of Morgannwg, which was to become Glamorgan, had fallen to the Normans, but Ifor Bach still held his chest out defiantly in parts of Senghenydd.

The Norman lord of the region was William Fitz Robert, Earl of Gloucester. Ifor, in essence, was a tenant of William, who held Cardiff Castle, and William was trying to take land which, under Welsh law, belonged to Ifor. Ifor Bach, short or not, scaled the walls of Cardiff Castle using his bare hands and kidnapped the Earl, his Countess, the daughter of the Earl of Leicester and their young son, Robert. He held them in the woods of Senghenydd and refused to release them until he had recovered his lost lands and a lot more. Descendants of Ifor Bach held sway in the area and harried the Normans for at least another century. Fair play to them.

If you travel along the M4 going east or west, where it

crosses the A470 in Cardiff North you view Castell Coch, built by the Marquis of Bute in the nineteenth century for his wife, who apparently only stayed there for three days. It is a folly, but it is reputed that Ifor Bach built a medieval castle on that site. Oh yes, Ifor was a six-cylinder warrior. What he lacked in height, he made up for in gusto unconfined and, when you think about it, what better mark on your achievements than to have a nightclub in Cardiff named after you? Clwb Ifor Bach is on Womanby Street in the Castle Quarter.

The land in the Upper Aber Valley, where Senghenydd has settled as the last village before you take the narrow moorland road to Nelson, was called The Park. It was a hunting ground, and encircling Senghenydd are the remains of this thirteenth-century gaming park, which was marked by a ditch and bank now known as the Senghenydd Dyke. It was well-stocked with game and deer and the private hunting ground of the de Clare family, builders and early occupants of Caerffili Castle, the second largest castle in terms of area in Britain. Long lengths of the dyke can still be seen today.

In fact, if you take the Aber Valley Heritage Trail, so many gems of the historical development of the area can be taken in. The thirteenth-century church of St Ilan and The Rose and Crown Pub at Eglwysilian have far-seeing viewpoints stretching to the channel in the south and the Brecon Beacons in the north. Other stopping places include the Windsor Colliery memorial at the edge of Abertridwr, and in Senghenydd the site of the Universal Colliery, the place that caused the village to be placed firmly in industrial history, the quest for coal and its heavy, awful, heart-rendering cost.

So we return to the 'What if?' question. In the 1880s, what would have happened here if Cardiff, as a large town, had gone ahead with plans to build a dam and drown the valley in a quest for water supply for its burgeoning population? It would have left a lake, a reservoir, viewed only by the inhabitants of the farming homesteads on the high valley slopes. Some of those farms are still there, having got used to the dramatic change in the valley since those peaceful years.

From that question we gradually come to the statement 'Lessons will be learnt!'

The sinking of the Universal Pit began in 1891; the York and Lancaster shafts went down almost 2000 feet. The west side districts below ground reflected the political times, with names like Pretoria, Mafeking, Kimberly and Ladysmith from the years of the Boer War. The pit attracted workers from all over Wales, all looking for employment.

When people talk of the Senghenydd explosion they usually mean the one in 1913, but there was an earlier one, a disastrous warm-up to the main event. It was in May 1913.

Idris Davies, the common man's poet from Rhymney, wrote in his poem *Gwalia Deserta*:

'Oh, what is man that coal should be so careless of him
And what is coal that so much blood be upon it?'

The first explosion was on 24th May 1901. Mercifully, if one can use such a word in these circumstances, it happened at the end of the night shift, when many of the miners had been brought to the surface. There were eighty-two left underground at the time of the explosion. Only one survived, saved when his horse was killed and fell against him, urinating upon him.

Oh yes, there was an enquiry. Professor Galloway of Cardiff University reported that fire, coal dust and air produced a deadly mixture which could be ignited without methane gas. Senghenydd was a hot, dry pit. Strong recommendations stated that owners of coal mines should ensure that all dusty roadways be thoroughly watered. In 1911, the Coal Mines Act listed a number of regulations to control electrical equipment to prevent sparking, the watering of dusty roadways and roofs and asserted that all mines should have reversible fans so that clean air could be provided in emergencies.

'Lessons will be learnt!' was the reassuring statement.

The Act demanded that all reversible fans be installed by 1st January 1913…but the mine owners at Senghenydd asked for and secured an extension, which was to run out on 16th September. Time was running out; by 14th October the fans were still not reversible.

It was 8.10 am that morning when the mine blew up and 439 men were killed, plus one rescuer. The huge blast took the two-ton cage shooting up the shaft, decapitating a banksman. Although the manager, Edward Shaw, showed bravery in going down the other shaft, there was a delay in calling the rescue services.

Of the seventeen charges brought against the manager, nine were dismissed. He was fined £24. It worked out at five and a half pence a miner, just over two pence in present-day money. The owners were fined £10, with £5.25 costs. Lord Merthyr, the main owner, died in August 1914 before sentence was passed.

The ravaging of the village and valley was almost beyond comprehension and the human suffering could never be truly calculated. It left 800 dependents, 205 widows, 542 children and 62 dependent fathers and mothers. Commercial Street lost forty-five men, High Street, on the ridge looking down on the Universal Pit site, lost thirty-five. Stanley Street lost nineteen, and the four terraces of Woodland, Cenydd, Graig and Phillips lost fifty-six. Mrs Elizabeth Twining of Commercial Street, who was made a widow a year before the disaster, lost three sons in it. Benjamin Priest of Ilan Road died with his two sons, Tommy, aged sixteen, and Jimmy, just fourteen.

It was the way of working underground, in family groups, that added to the closely related casualties. For many years, the working practices and payment arrangements continued. If a man was on an eight-hour shift and was killed just three hours into the shift, then no payment was credited for the hours not worked.

The story continued in so many houses. The funerals, when they started, were dramatic and harrowing in their sheer numbers as they travelled slowly to the graveyards of Eglwysilian and Penyrheol. On many of the gravestones, in Welsh, was inscribed:

'Be farw yn Nhanchwa Senghenydd.' – 'He died in the Senghenydd explosion'.

So many of those lost had their origins in the far-off

corners of Wales. There is the story of a letter written by a man of the north to his friend back home in Bethesda.

Written in his native tongue, in English it reads: 'Here I am after some time of silence, still alive. I'm working in Senghenydd...the best pit in the world.' The letter was received on 14th October 1913. The explosion had happened an hour before.

Senghenydd was still a young village, one of many industrial villages to spring up during the mid and late 1800s. In Senghenydd in 1880, the valley was overlooked only by the farmsteads on the ridges. By the 1890s the melting pot was coming to the boil and men and boys coursed their life's blood to carve the coal seamed Klondikes into new communities. Vibrant of spirit and searching of soul, they set up, in time, the keystones of society, in their clubs, institutes, halls, libraries, hospitals and chapels from wage contributions. In the constant quest for coal, so many paid the ultimate price; some in mind-numbing numbers, others on their own and others in small groups. Gleision Colliery, with its loss of four men in September 2011 was not a disaster, according to agreed assessments. A disaster, officially, in mining terms, has to be five men or more.

The memorial at Senghenydd has been adopted as the National Mining Memorial. Circled around it are paviers naming every mining disaster in Welsh history, the name of the pit, the name of the village, the date of the explosion and the number of men and boys killed: Abercarn, 1894, 268 men lost; Gresford, 1934, 266 lost; Ferndale, 1867, 178 lost; Llanerch Abersychan, 1890, 176 lost, and so the list goes on. In 1892, 112 men and boys died at Parc Slip Aberkenfig. There they worked endlessly, over months, to bring all the bodies out and, in a measure of love for man and the working creatures beside them, the bodies of fifteen horses were carried out, leaving only one which they couldn't reach.

At Albion Colliery, Cilfynydd, in 1894, 290 died, along with 123 horses, an almost forgotten disaster, yet the second biggest in terms of fatalities. Horses were counted carefully in many instances, because horses had to be bought, unlike men. The full list would make a long chapter of poigancy.

I was accorded the privilege of a small underground tour of the Albion Colliery before the site was cleared. Pontypridd High School now stands on the site of the mine, just off the A470 on Cilfynydd Common.

Add the horror of 1966, the tip slide at Aberfan, to the harrowing list: 144 killed, 116 of them schoolchildren, on the Friday before a half-term holiday, and the accumulated ravage of communities becomes a screaming rage. A disaster and an unforgivable man-made abomination.

Senghenydd shares a brotherhood with so many other communities, a brotherhood of pride amidst the the soul-touching sadness, pain and cost of the quest for black gold that brought such vibrancy and danger to the communities in The Valleys.

There is so much of history, in layers, in the Aber Valley. Do visit. Feel the passage of years as you wander the hillsides, treading the Senghenydd Dyke, follow the Aber Valley trail, turn the pages of the past, look down on the site of the Universal Pit and quietly consider what went on there.

So, finally, we come to the third episode of the village drawing me in. I was asked back to be a part of the 100th anniversary commemoration of the 1913 explosion. It was a privilege to stand at the memorial and relate the Senghenydd story. Apparently, the villagers felt I qualified. I had played rugby there, I had taught there, and my own grandfather had been killed in a coal mine, the Steer Pit in Gwaun Cae Gurwen. I remember that day well. I was seven years of age.

When you visit and follow the Aber Valley Trail and sense the Senghenydd story, in the stillness on the slope, looking down past the four terraces and towards High Street, think, if you will, of 8.10 a.m. on the morning of 14th October 2013: 100 years exactly to when Senghenydd was writ large and sorrowfully into Welsh history. It was at that time precisely, during the moving yet inspirational commemorative service, that an eerie sound was heard, moving like an unseen gathering through the years. With thousands of people on the valley slopes, all as one in thought and quiet contemplation, the original Universal Pit hooter mournfully blasted out again three times, as it had done on that fateful morning in 1913.

8. The Elephant and the Highwayman

Ceredigion

When I worked on the Llandeilo District Council 'muck gang' during the long summer holidays of my student days, the gang was often sent to remote areas or lonely villages on the north Carmarthenshire and Ceredigion border.

Our foreman was Trevor from Penygroes, a man with a strong back, far-seeing thought, and a straight tongue that fired bullets of common sense. He had fought his way through Sicily and up the entire leg of Italy during the Second World War on just one word of 'needs-must' Italian: *Quanto?* – How much? In cutting a trench on council business, we students would sometimes get very keen.

'Hey Trevor, we can finish this trench and close it in before the end of the week.'

'No, boys, where's your sense? We've got to save a length for Monday or they'll send us somewhere else.'

Another piece of his foresight comes to mind: 'Remember now boys, if we're digging a trench on any sloping ground, always throw the muck up the slope. Then, when we come to re-fill it, we'll only have to kick the muck in...downhill, a dawdle.'

Trevor had two lieutenants. The first was Gwyn Trapp, who took his name from the village of his birth, Trapp, near Llandeilo. He was the lorry driver and always wore a black beret. The other was Bob Eak, who had been full-time temporary on the Llandeilo Council for at least fifteen years and was a poet on the long-armed shovel. Watching his movements in slide, push, lift, flick, throw and repeat was a kind of ballet, art in action.

I remember a stint in the northern reaches of the Towy Valley, outside the village of Cil-y-Cwm, near Llandovery. We were digging a trench for a pipe connection from the main water supply to what appeared to be a mini-mansion in renovation. For this job, we had been promoted from 'muck gang' to 'water gang'; no extra pay, but a lot of kudos.

Up the lane and 'round the bend was the road to Rhandirmwyn, a name synonymous with the Welsh Robin Hood, Twm Siôn Cati. A man of folklore, elasticated legend and a measure of mystical myth. His bolthole was in Rhandirmwyn, his hidden safe haven, but his playground as a thief and highwayman was to the west, over the hills to Tregaron, where he was born. Tregaron, the base for this romantic roustabout and also, in later times, the place of another mystery: the missing elephant. You may think an elephant, being so large, is not easy to mislay, especially in a place which just edges over the line from village to town, but they have managed to do it.

According to verified tales, in 1848 Batty's travelling menagerie visited Tregaron as part of its seasonal round of towns in Wales. A young elephant was taken ill, having drunk more than a drop of contaminated water, so it is said, and died. He was sadly and duly buried, but where? That is the question. An archaeological search in 2011 found nothing. It was rumoured that the elephant was buried in the back garden of the town's Talbot Inn. So, 'Jwmbi', as it's known locally, is still missing. The Talbot Hotel, a thirteenth-century hostelry, once owned one hundred acres, so another survey, over a wider area, might glean success.

I have fond memories of The Talbot. I stayed there after speaking at the annual dinner of Tregaron RFC. I well remember being woken up by the sound of revelry in the town square and saw from my front window a few bucks of the parish gathering outside the Spar shop, waiting for it to open so that a kind of breakfast could be obtained.

Tregaron is historic, an old drovers' stopover, a weekly market town, and the hub of an area that borders the Desert of Wales, so called because it is generally inaccessible, devoid of many tracks and roads and largely uninhabited by humans. It is clearly not a dry desert, in that it has heavy rainfall, and a more accurate title for it is the Green Desert of Wales. The expanse corresponds, roughly, to the upland area named Elenydd in Welsh and is more commonly known as the Cambrian Mountains.

The church is dedicated to St Caron, a man of lowly origins, but his courage obtained for him the sovereignty of Wales. He had a real go at the Romans, reigned for seven years and, on passing, was buried in Tregaron.

The area, too, has the distinction of having the remotest chapel in the whole of Wales. Built of rubble stone from ruined farmhouses and large pebbles from a river bed, the Calvanistic Methodist chapel stands whitewashed and proud on its lonely spot, situated in the Cambrian Mountains, on the road between Tregaron and the vast, watery expanse of Llyn Brianne, the reservoir near Rhandirmwyn. 'Soar y Mynydd', 'Zoar of the Mountain', derived its name from the mention in Genesis which served as a sanctuary for Lot and his daughters, and which was spared by God when the cities of Sodom and Gomorrah were destroyed. Its congregation had fallen to two by 1968, but in 1973 its status was secured and some well-attended services are now held in the summer months.

To the north of Tregaron is Gors Caron or Tregaron Bog, fertile land when drained and known for its adders, buzzards, red kites and polecats. To the west is a hilly region with self-sufficient hill farmers on smallholdings. Some of these families have farmed the land for centuries over the generations.

When I was in the sixth form of Amman Valley Grammar School, my main love was geography, with history being a close fellow traveller. One summer, Evans Geog, our teacher, arranged an adventure for us. We were to head out of Ammanford for Aberystwyth, with our rural route on a loop taking in Tregaron and Pontrhydfendigaid. The bus would pull in at a remote farm in the Cambrian Mountains where lived two bachelor brothers. It was a refreshment stop and whilst there we were to take a close look at the brothers' heads, without staring. Allegedly, the brothers had a bloodline that took them back to the Bronze Age with very little pollution of their vessels and with little or no mixing of blood. The bike probably put an end to all that, but they must have had a horse or two as transport, so I couldn't understand it. However, there it was and there they were. In fact, we were later told that the brothers had agreed that, on passing on, their skulls would be donated to medical research. They were known as Pumlumon Man and in the 1950s and 1960s it was common for experts to visit the area, carrying callipers with which to measure their skulls, but this fell out of favour. How they put up with it I don't know.

Now, a confession. There were other areas in Wales where the inhabitants had bloodlines going back to the ancients. One was my home patch, where resided Brynaman Man or Black Mountain Man. Before DNA, it was found through research by Aberystwyth University and callipers, that there were still a few Bronze Age descendents living there. I've often wondered about one or two boys in the village. Even the pack of forwards playing for Brynaman Rugby Club are stocky and earthy, very short but very vibrant.

Notables of Tregaron over the centuries included Joseph Jenkins, the Welsh swagman, who proved that a mid-life crisis is not a new phenomenon. He was judged, in 1857, to have the best farm in Cardiganshire, yet in 1869 he suddenly left his life on the land, his eisteddfod winning poetry, his wife and family and shot off to Australia. No doubt he camped at many a billabong, underneath the shade of a coolibah tree, waiting till his billy boiled, hell-bent on waltzing Matilda at the opportune moment. Twenty-five years later he returned, no doubt carrying a convincing absence note and many volumes of diaries. They were discovered seventy years later in the attic of one of his descendants and have become an important Australian historical text.

Another son of Tegaron was Henry Richard, known as the Apostle of Peace. Born in this part of Wales but nurtured in London, he was an uncompromising non-conformist pacifist. In 1879 he remarked that Britain had waged seventy-three wars in sixty-three years, including the Chinese Opium Wars and the Boer and Afghan wars. Although a successful minister, in 1868 he became the Liberal MP for Merthyr Tydfil and Aberdare, a seat he held for twenty years.

So, to the Welsh Robin Hood, Twm Siôn Cati, who roamed the wild ranges, a vagabond and thief with guile and style, if folklore is to be believed.

Born on the other side of the blanket, as it were, he was the illegitimate son of Cati Jones of Tregaron and was named Thomas. His father, who had kept Cati warm in winter, and most other seasons, was supposed to be Siôn ap Dafydd ap Madog ap Hywel Moetheu, of Porth–y-ffin. That is the way with the Welsh. Simple surnames are cast over hedges and into ditches and 'ap', signifying 'son of', ensures a long pedigree and a confusion in the mind. In the end you don't very easily know who's related to who, even as brother and sister, so it really is walking in a field of eggs when speaking out of turn about anyone...they could be family.

Another oral tale, since written down, marks Twm as the illegitimate son of Cati and John Wynn of Gwydir, John Wynn ap Maredudd, as known. He was to become a gentleman farmer and, according to some, a herald bard of his day, but in his youth a womaniser of varying success and clearly, as agreed, a notorious outlaw. Either Cati was a warm, welcoming woman, or the oral tales, told with a jug of ale in front of a roaring, night-settling fire, added colourful and entrancing mileage to the unfolding saga.

Further adding to the mix, it was also common practice in rural Wales, traditionally a matriarchal society, for children with common names to be nicknamed after their mothers. So Thomas became Twm Siôn Cati.

He was supposedly a Protestant, not a safe religious commitment when Mary I, a Catholic, was on the throne. So, marked as a rebel, he decided to go the whole hog and chose robbery as a means of employment. It was also said that for a while he fled to Geneva in 1557 to escape the law, returning two years later when Elizabeth I, a Protestant, gained the throne. Geneva, to be fair, seems a long hop for safety. With guile and geography, the nooks and crannies around Pontrhydfendigaid would have been a cheaper option.

Stories abound of his skill, his methods, and his flair and tricks in the outlaw art. There are so many that one has to ask if they can all be attributed to the same man. He was the Scarlet Pimpernel of the Green Desert, Tregaron and its hinterland. Some have reported that he robbed the rich and gave to the poor, very much like the mythical Robin Hood. Others suggest that both Robin and Twm robbed anyone who had a few bob, irrespective of status and depth of means.

One event centres on a farmer hunting Twm after the theft of a bullock. The farmer reaches Twm's mother's house and asks whether Twm Siôn Cati lives there. A beggar, by looks, answers the door and says, 'Yes, he lives here, I'll hold your horse and whip while you go in.' No sooner is he in than the beggar, Twm himself, jumps onto the horse. He gallops to the farmer's house and tells the farmer's wife that the farmer is in trouble, needs money urgently and has sent Twm to fetch it. The farmer's wife pays up and Twm, in possession of the horse, whip and the money, hastily departs for London, sells the horse and is quids in. It has the mark of being an early prototype of a telephone banking scam or cold caller, when you think about it.

There are many such stories, but he is perhaps best remembered for the sensitive treatment he metered out to his victims. Twm avoided killing them; he is reputed to have been able to fire an arrow which would pin his victim to the saddle of his horse, leaving them helpless but generally unharmed except for the immediate onset of stress, which they wouldn't recognise because that modern-day affliction had not been invented yet.

According to stories picked up at the time, between the ages of eighteen and nineteen, in order to free himself and his mother from the poverty they had long endured, he adopted the profession of full-blooded thief and became celebrated not only in his own area and domain but throughout Wales.

Twm often hid from his arch enemy, the Sheriff of Carmarthen, on the slopes of the densely wooded and rugged Dinas Hill, north of Llandovery, close to the village of Rhandirmwyn. The river Pysgotwr, 'Fisherman', joins the upper Towy and roars through the gorge.

That area today is an RSPB nature reserve and a footpath runs around the hill, with a branch leading to Twm Siôn Cati's cave.

Later in life, this rogue, but a loveable one, the hero of legends, is said to have changed his ways, married an heiress of Ystradffin and lived in a grand house near

Tregaron, becoming wealthy and a Justice of the Peace. He had great qualifications for seeing through any criminals brought before him.

If you visit Rhandirmwyn there are hostelries for the weary traveller, especially if you seek out Twm's bolthole, the secret cave, The Royal Oak in the village itself and, across the River Towy, the Towy Bridge Inn.

If you visit Tregaron, there are a few good watering wells within striking distance of the town, but do call in at The Talbot, have some sustenance, and if you happen to have a dousing stick and the gift, seek out the elephant. It's beginning to attain the folklore status of Twm himself.

9. Iechyd Da from Tredegar

Tredegar

In Scotland, there is, allegedly, somewhere on a hillside, a large standing stone that should be registered with the National Health Service. Stories circulate that if you have an ailment or a vexing illness, you should seek out the stone, approach it, and give it a prolonged hug.

The base of the stone, well below ground, must clearly be in touch with the primeval elements and a positively charged ley line that exudes life enhancing bursts of nature's 'feel good' electricity. After hugging the pillar for a given period, however long is comfortable for you, you should experience some relief. Of course, depending on the severity of your physical complaint, you might need a full course of visits and hugs and, inevitably these days, there may be a waiting list for appointments.

Having read about this phenomenon, I naturally asked the question on my radio programme: 'Was there such a stone in Wales?' I did not have to wait long for a reply.

'The Blue Stones of the Preseli Mountains in the west, Roy. If you visit the area, lay on the stones overnight and if you don't die of hypothermia, you'll be fine and ready for a full breakfast in the morning.'

Now the Preseli region is a special area, but I had not heard of the health enhancing bonuses that go with it. I have visited the Gwaun Valley in the Preseli Range many times and it does have the feel of a parallel universe about it. The inhabitants did not change to the Julian calender in 1752, being comfortable with the Gregorian time span. Even now, New Year's Eve, or *Calenig*, is celebrated on 13th January. The school children get an unofficial day off school so that they can go 'round the houses singing New

Year carols in exchange for treats and sweets.

In the Gwaun Valley is the Dyffryn Arms, known by all who pass that way as Bessie's Pub. It used to be named the Llwyn Celyn, the Holly Bush, and it has been owned by Bessie's family since 1845. When you enter, I swear you slip through a portal to another time and space. It is very mid-nineteenth-century, like sitting in someone's front room. I don't know if it's changed, but I recall a hatch with Bessie, in mittens, serving cask ale from somewhere to her left. Nineteenth-century ambience, twenty-first century prices, which is fair enough, lest the excise people query arrangements.

A visit there will definitely enhance your well being, without the extra chore of having to lie on one of the famed Blue Stones. A few pints as a dose and your pain should ease. Either that, or you simply won't care or worry about it.

Incidentally, the Gwaun Valley is one of the most important melt-water channels of the last Ice Age, so its connection with the life enhancing properties of the ancients is on tap.

Moving east to the Heads of the Valleys, there are standing stones with notable connections to health cover and community support for the inhabitants. They are the Aneurin Bevan Stones, four pillars in all. If you take the old road through Duke's Town, between Tredegar and Ebbw Vale, turn into the site at the summit of the hill. It's alongside the A465, now dualled in that section, the famed Yellow Brick Road that travels with you from Abergavenny to Neath.

Not too far away is the large, low rock of rough-hewn sandstone commemorating the men of Gwent who fought against Fascism in the Spanish Civil War and Second World War.

The four Aneurin Bevan stones, surrounded by a small, dry moat, define the place where Aneurin Bevan stood to address his followers. His name is on one, but the other three face the valleys that were part of his patch and base: Rhymney, Sirhowy and Ebbw.

Bevan, in his speeches, no doubt mentioned his dream to support the weak and sick. To provide free health care at the point of need, a National Health Service for the UK. This was no far-off vision or pipe dream. He and his fellow councillors had already set up a scheme in his home town of Tredegar.

The model was the local community self-help scheme run by Tredegar Workmen's Medical Aid Society, on which Bevan had served as a committee member in the 1920s. 'All I am doing is extending to the entire population of Britain the benefits we had in Tredegar for a generation or more. We are going to "Tredegar-ise you."' He never would have imagined how it has expanded today from its launch in 1948, when he was Minister of Health.

It is extraordinary how, over the years, we have taken it for granted; health is second only to the weather in opening a conversation. 'Nice day for it. Cold for the time of year, isn't it?' Then, when we feel confident to proceed, in comes: 'How's it going? Lot of 'flu about, grabs you in the chest I feel. I try and avoid travelling by bus because of all the people coughing.'

Health cover of old had a back-up system: grandmothers, and, an endangered species these days, aunties. There aren't as many aunties about as in my day. I lived in a street of fifteen houses and over half of them were aunties, some, admittedly, were surrogates who lived as close neighbours. I remember one of my far-flung aunties, Auntie Katie from Port Talbot. She always dressed in black and loved funerals. She gloried in being a spinster because that meant she had free rein, she said. I was told later in life that she'd had her chances of marriage; there was a curate from Baglan who was very keen, but he got fed up and went off with an usherette from the Albert Hall in Swansea.

She once trapped me in the kitchen of my grandmother's house. 'Listen,' she said, 'take some advice now for your own good. If you wash your hair, don't go to bed for an hour, or you'll get the pillow wet and you'll catch a cold. Another thing, take your vest off on May 31st, and, whatever the weather, put it back on as soon as October knocks at the door. And...and...being that you're a boy, don't cross your legs until you're fifteen years of age, alright?' On reflection, I wish I'd listened to her now.

Funny how the old remedies stick. If you had a carbuncle, the skin inside a boiled egg was good to draw it out and bring it to a head. Golden Eye ointment was a regular in the cupboard, along with cotton wool, which you used for snow on your windows at Christmas. I haven't seen a good sty on the eye for years, so I haven't seen too much Golden Eye ointment either. A sore throat was remedied with warm goose grease and a woman's silk stocking wound 'round your neck.

Visits to the doctor were a lottery. You didn't want to go to the surgery on a Monday. It was packed then, because Monday was 'paper day'; when men could get a doctor's paper to have a few days off work. There were regulars there every Monday, the doctor knew them intimately; in fact, if the regulars didn't show, the doctor thought they were bad...ill, or something.

The surgeries were so crowded and the walls so thin between the waiting room and consulting room that, unless a lorry or a bus was passing, everyone knew which ointment was going where and why.

Our doctor was Dr Warner, from Ireland. A lovely man who sought a second opinion straight away if he wasn't sure. He'd send you to outpatients in Swansea. The nursing sister in charge in outpatients was of direct lineage to Boudicca, who didn't take any truck from the Romans. 'Where are you from? Who's your doctor? Who did you say? Well, there's no point in sending for records then.' Dr Warner had one weakness...a wayward and cavalier record system. But, he'd sent you to hospital just to check things out, so you reckoned you were in safe hands.

In hospital, there was a regimented routine established. No children were allowed in the wards at visiting time, so, visiting my grandfather, I had to be held up to the window to see him. Only two visitors to a bed. If you were three and Matron was due, you'd soon scamper to a bed with one visitor, or none at all, and have a chat with someone you didn't know. Even as a patient, if Matron was due on the ward you had to lie ill tidily. No creases or bumps were tolerated on the blankets.

Now here's a throwback of an idea to remedy modern day bed-blocking: convalescent homes. After a few days in a hospital, following treatment, you were sent to a convalescent home. Bed-blocking avoided and you were still in care, but not critical. Very civilized, I always thought.

Dentists remain in the memory vividly. When the school dentist came around, the girls were given pink forms and the boys blue ones. What you didn't want after the initial examination was a yellow card. That meant you had to get treatment. Sometimes, that treatment was in the school. I hated having gas for a tooth extraction. That awful flat metal gob-stopper was put in your mouth and as the gas took hold your mind would spin tighter and tighter, until you heard a crack...and then you'd come round, bleeding into a bowl.

I once attended a dentist in school who was doing fillings when the electricity failed. He had a few boys peddle like mad on a static wheel to keep the drill spinning. I've never gripped the handles of any chair as tightly as I did that day.

So, to the kick-off of the National Health Service, Tredegar was the scout before the wagon train. The local initiative went back to 1890 and a merger of various local societies in Tredegar to form the Tredegar Workmen's Medical Aid and Sick Relief Fund, later to become the Tredegar Workmen's Medical Aid Society. The local Cottage Hospital was established in 1904 and by 1911 the Society was well regarded nationally, far in advance of other societies. By 1933 the Society was supplying the medical needs of ninety-five per cent of the local population, with five doctors, two dentists with a mechanic each, pharmacy dispensers and assistants, and a nurse. To be fair, it has to be said that the doctors were allowed some private work, which was again a model taken on by the National Health Service

Tredegar holds a hallowed place in the health of the nation, then, though the town could be celebrated for several developments. It was a hotbed of socialist politics and a cornerstone of the Industrial Revolution. It had several fine buildings in the town, many of which survive and can be visited, such as Bedwellty House. Add the famed town clock and it is all worth a visit. On the down side, three serious riots occurred there too, named the Election, the Irish and the Jewish riots, but they are for another chapter, in another book. For the present, good health and good cheer are to the forefront of our ponderings.

Of course, there is the quandary about the name. Tredegar was originally thought to come from the Welsh 'Tre deg erw', the town of ten acres, or 'Tri deg erw', thirty acres, but it is now thought to originate from the time Samuel Homfray, who started an iron works in the town, married into the Morgan family based at Coedcernyw, near Newport. The family home was Tredegar House, which can be seen from the M4 and is synonymous with Captain Henry Morgan, the buccaneer. It was because of that connection that Homfray named his iron works the Tredegar Iron Company, and the town's name followed. A fillip to the name is the fact that the historic Tredegar Ironworks in Richmond, Virginia, in the United States, is, of course, named after the original, ours, at the top of the Sirhowy Valley.

Oddly, on the Morgan connection, there is an attractive park north of the town, Parc Bryn Bach, and I was told, admittedly in a hostelry late of an evening, that Henry Morgan had buried some of his ill-gotten gains on the land where the park and the lake are now situated. Very unlikely, but it all adds to the mysticism.

From shipping and pirating to flying. On an OS map of the area, there is an aircraft runway marked near the park, not far from the route of the Yellow Brick Road, the A465. Why? Don't ask. It can be just seen, they say, especially if it has been snowing. In no other way is it marked, not by a small control tower or by a standing stone...a stone, perhaps, to indicate an aid to good health for someone trying to land safely in the wintry mists of the surrounding Heads of the Valleys moorland and trying, desperately, to avoid potholes and sheep.

10. To the Sea, Scholarship and Illtud's Place

Llantwit Major

It was on a cold January in 1968 that it happened, without warning...my first attack of rampant hypochondria. I was on my 'have chalk, will travel' tour of temporary teaching appointments in south Glamorgan since my return from what we termed missionary work in England.

Actually, my two years in Bath had been very enjoyable and in ex-mining country in Radstock, north Somerset, the college stint at lecturing had been very good for me.

Now, here I was, in my final furlong before marriage, in Llantwit Major, booked in for digs with Mrs Pearce at a longhouse called The Curriers, which, apparently, had once been a pub. It was opposite the post office in the town. The trouble was, I was locked out. I wasn't to know that Mrs Pearce had regular habits, one being a visit to the Old White Hart down in the town square for two bottles of nightly Mackenson stout. It was a cold night and I was somehow instinctively drawn to the Old White Hart. There she was, Mrs Pearce, my landlady for the next six months.

She was a lovely lady and The Curriers was listed as a local B&B. Police would often call there at night with wayward and weary travellers looking for shelter.

In January, I found my bedroom cold. My part en-suite was a jug and a bowl on the sideboard. A visit to the toilet was an orienteering trip. It required the turning on of six light switches, the opening of three doors and an amble or a jog down to the bottom of the garden to the personal comfort cabin.

It was then that it hit, on the first night: hypochondria. For some illogical reason, I thought my bed was damp, so I put on several layers. Vest, old fashioned winceyette pyjamas, rugby jersey, track suit, scarf and Dai cap, which I carried for emergencies only. I also ripped up all the brochures advertising exotic honeymoon places so that I could stuff the pages in the gaps in the windows to stop the drafts. I'd read somewhere that one of the most comfortable ways to die was in snow, or in extreme cold. The danger signs are when you start to feel warm, comfortable and sleepy, so I tried to stay awake, just in case.

I was alive in the morning and, my word, wasn't the breakfast magnificent. I couldn't kick the habit though. Every night I went through the same routine at bedtime. By the beginning of February I was convinced I was ailing and had to seek medical help. The doctor was very reassuring and more of a psychologist really. After examining me he said, 'Look, there's nothing physically wrong with you. Anyway, you have too many pains in too many places for it to be serious. Is there anything in your life that is unusual, or is there an event that's filling your mind with plans or concerns?'

'Not really,' I replied, 'but I'm getting married on 1st August.'

'Ah, there you are then,' responded the doc smugly. 'Listen, by 1st August all these pains will go, disappear. You mark my words. I'll give you some tablets to tide you over for a week, for your body to calm down, but don't drink alcohol after taking them, mind.' And so it proved to be.

By the way, with any other health issues I had, I was advised by the locals to go to the pharmacist. He was 'old school' and should have been given an honorary medical degree just from his life's experience. He could diagnose many an ailment as you walked up the step to the shop and, so I was told, he was usually spot on. I saw many such health-purveying soothsayers over the years. Quite a few were just as good with animals as humans, sometimes concocting their own remedy in the back room of the shop.

I had arrived in Llantwit Major via the A48, the east to west express way and ley line in south Wales before the M4 arrived. I had travelled from the west, the Port Talbot side, so not exactly a wise man from the east in education or teaching terms. I had stopped on the Golden Mile, a name that always intrigued me, and, on enquiry, I've been given so many 'truths' as to the reason for the title. A roundabout has been placed on the stretch now, so it's spoilt a bit, but locals still maintain that the original Golden Mile was a mile or so west of the village of Pentre Meyrick.

The story suggests that the name goes back to a time when the Prince of Glamorgan, Iestyn ap Gwrgant, was always at loggerheads with his neighbour, Rhys ap Tewdwr. He got fed up of being hard-pressed and sought the help of the Norman godfather of the area, Baron Fitzhamon. Iestyn sent a trusted follower, Einon ap Einon, to see the Baron, on a promise that if he was successful he could have Iestyn's daughter in marriage. The Baron agreed to the request, but only on payment of a mile of gold.

With their combined force they defeated Rhys, who was chased to Hirwaun, probably the one near Pyle, not Aberdare, before they got him. As agreed, the Norman soldiers lined the route and the coins, so it is said, were laid out in a line before them. However, Iestyn broke his promise to Einon, who was not given Iestyn's daughter in marriage. Einon returned to the Baron and suggested that, for spite, they now join forces and have a go at Iestyn. So it came to pass, and it was Iestyn's turn to do the sprinting in retreat, to no avail; he did not get to his next birthday.

Another version of how the Golden Mile came to be so called centres on a drover who once was driving his cattle to London via the Vale Of Glamorgan and decided to stop for a rest near a shady nook. Once there, he was surprised to see a fox creeping towards him. The fox had a grey appearance and a worried look upon his face. More concerning for the drover was the point when the fox started speaking, saying that he was distressed and had many burdens. Pulling himself together, the drover started laughing and the fox became angry, shouting that he was really Einon ap Einon, who had betrayed the Welsh and Iestyn ap Tewdwr to the Normans. As a punishment he was doomed to spend eternity as a fox.

Allegedly, the legend persists and in many Welsh county and country areas the fox is seen as the devil's spy. To see several foxes together means you should avoid buying a lottery ticket for a week or so, and to see a dark or black fox, or a white fox or grey fox, well...don't ask.

I think I'll go with the original story of the Normans being paid on that mile and discard the afterthoughts as folklore elastic.

I left the A48 near Pentre Meyrick and headed for the sea to seek out my digs, hopefully without any foxes caught in my headlights. There I'd meet Mrs Pearce and wander the streets of Llantwit Major.

Llantwit Major has been inhabited for 3000 years, occupied from Neolithic times, and in the beach area are the remains of an Iron Age fort. The Romans set up shop too with a villa at Caer Mead, suggesting that it was a controlled, quiet area in their time of occupation. After the clarion call came to return to defend the Roman Empire in the fifth century, the years passed and St Illtyd entered the scene, creating the great seat of learning around about the year 500 A.D., so they say. In the 1960s, of course, we teachers felt that we were continuing the great learning depth and tradition, perhaps not on such a grand scale, but we did our bit...

The village primary school was right next door to The Curriers and the secondary school was out on the Boverton Road, but my educational establishment was St Illtyd's School, which catered for the children from the large RAF camp at St Athan.

I was happy there.

The town's name in Welsh is Llanilltud Fawr, Illtud's Greater Church, as opposed to, say, Llantwit Fardre, Llanilltud Faerdref in Welsh, which I suppose, knows its place in the St Illtud pecking order. Saint Illtud originally came to the area from Brittany. He founded the monastery of Illtud and the college attached to it, the Seminary of Theodosius, Cor Tewdws in Welsh, which grew into one of the esteemed Christian colleges of the times. Scholars came from across Wales, Devon, Cornwall and Brittany.

At its peak, it reputedly had 7 halls, over 400 houses and more than 2000 students, including seven sons of British princes and scholars such as St Patrick, St Paul and the poet Taliesin, amongst many others. Impressive place. Even St David is believed to have spent some time there. That is some alumni, let's be fair, a gold top past students register.

The area did suffer its trials and tests of faith in succumbing to invasions by those who had a different educational curriculum. In turn the Saxons, Danes and Vikings, great believers in geography, outdoor environmental studies and PE, extreme physical exercise, caused mayhem, the Vikings destroying the place in the year 987. The Normans repeated the exercise in the eleventh century. However, in the year 1111, it is documented as being restored, at least in part. It did function as a monastic school until the sixteenth-century Reformation.

Unfortunately, nothing remains of the original monastery, but the present church was originally built between 950 and 1400, so there is that incredible historic link.

Whether you stay in or roam through Llantwit Major, you cannot fail to feel the mantle of history all about you. Take in the square around the War Memorial, originally a preaching cross with a date set in Tudor times, the Old White Hart, a sixteenth-century building but an eighteenth-century inn, as well as the Old Swan Inn, once thatched, where a building has stood since the eleventh century. It has been used as a private mint twice, once as a monastic or manorial mint and later for private enterprise. For a period it was a private house for the influential Stradling family of St Donats. To assure present-day balance I should mention that there are five other pubs and four restaurants in the town.

Down the hill, Church Street leads to St Illtud's Church, on a site which has seen Christian worship for over 1500 years. On the hill above the church is the medieval grange, a large farm on land given to Tewkesbury Abbey. The only surviving buildings are the gatehouse and a dovecote. Nearby are the original police station and the row of cottages known as Hillhead, built originally to house the poor. Now, it must be here that the ruins of the original school were located...or not? Worth checking though. You can also pass a ruin on the western edge of the town, usually known as the Old Place (it dates from 1596 but was only occupied for about a hundred years) and on the northern end of the old town stands the Great House, Ty Mawr or Upper House, a superb example of a Tudor town house. There are so many listed buildings in the town that they would fill a formidable catalogue. The best place to start investigating is the Information Centre in the Town Hall, which is a sixteenth-century building. Oddly, the so-called Town Hall, originally a court house, was never actually a town hall at all.

There's so much history in the very air and ambience of the place, but I'll tell you when I felt it at its most powerful. It was during springtime and one of my evening walks down the lane and 'round the bend. Well, more than one bend really, but the lane straightened and led you towards the shore. The Afon Colhuw meanders with you and discharges through an outfall into the sea. The beach is pebbled and the cliffs either side of the flat Colhugh Valley are steep and unstable. The rocks have fine examples of

Jurassic period fossils, but great care must be taken on the cliff walks to St Donat's Castle and Atlantic College, for dramatic erosion has taken place in recent years.

The feeling of treading in the footsteps of time struck me at its strongest on that walk along the lane from the town to the shore and, as evening gathered me close, the return journey filled my thoughts and musings with questions. Who has walked this way before? 3000 years of habitation, the scholars from the ancient school of saints and princes, the destroying invader from the sea.

I feel the same way when I tread a Roman road, a drovers' way or mountain track, marked not by sheep but by man. When you think about it, we are only passing through and it is as well, now and again, to dwell on it. Too often we take our close surroundings, our familiar community and the homeland we think we know for granted. History, in its different chapters, is all about us and our geography and sense of place...always there for seeing, accepting and appreciating.

I have only touched upon Llantwit Major with a light brush, so I'll take my palette and move on, inland, to Cowbridge.

11. The 'Cow-bridge'

Vale of Glamorgan

The road from Llantwit Major to Cowbridge passes through Llandow aerodrome. Many of the hangers are still in place, on both sides of the road. It was the site, in 1950, of the world's worst air disaster at that time. The Avro Tudor V, named *Star Girl*, carrying rugby fans and supporters home from an international match in Dublin, crashed in clear weather while trying to land. The plane, initially booked for seventy-two passengers, had been stripped to accommodate another six seats. The total death toll was eighty. There were three survivors. Two, who walked away unaided, had been sitting in additional seats bolted in the back, and a third man, who was in the toilet, was knocked unconscious but lived. An investigation concluded that the cause of the crash was the loading of the aircraft, which had moved the centre of gravity considerably aft of where it should have been. Most people these days, in the nature of fading memory or having no knowledge of it all, pass the site without a glance or second thought. It was world news at the time.

Cowbridge saw another air crash in the same year. A Bristol freighter, on a test flight from Bristol Filton Airport, developed structural failure and crashed near the town, killing the four men aboard.

A couple of miles down the road and 'round a bend, you pass Crossways as you near Cowbridge itself. When I was employed, on my travels as a temporary teacher, I was in digs in Crossways. It was the home of lovely people, Mr and Mrs Shepherd and Mrs Shepherd's sister, Miss Lawrence, who lived in a large caravan in their garden.

The Shepherds had worked in service in London,

consequently there was a knock on my bedroom door at seven o'clock every morning, a cup of tea and a biscuit was delivered and my shoes were taken away to be cleaned. The breakfasts were sumptuous and the evening meal was always three courses. I can still taste the custard with added cloves now. In the two terms I was in Cowbridge Grammar School I put on two stone in weight, even after trying to walk to school most mornings on the back road through the lovely village of Llanblethian to compensate for the meals.

Cowbridge lies on the site of a Roman settlement, identified by scholars as 'Bovium', cow place. There are seventeenth-century references to a 'cow-bridge' over the town's river, the Thaw, but the Welsh name for Cowbridge is Y Bont-faen, the stone bridge.

The town is still sitting on its medieval plan, with one long street divided into burgage plots, land in tenure for yearly rents. Substantial sections of the town wall and the South Gate are still standing. They were built in the thirteenth century, after Richard de Clare became head kingpin in the region. He extended his domain to include several surrounding villages.

Serious Welsh influence and pressure occurred in 1403, when King Henry IV of England battled the roving Owain Glyndŵr. Details of the outcome are scant, but the site of the battle has been recognised by Cadw for inclusion in a Register of Historic Battlefields in Wales.

Iolo Morgannwg, inventor and designer of the present day rituals of the National Eisteddfod of Wales, kept a bookshop in the High Street. There is a plaque there now inscribed with the eisteddfodic words *Y Gwir yn erbyn y Byd*, 'Truth against the World'. Iolo apparently held the first meeting of the Gorsedd, the assembly of bards, just outside the town in 1795.

The present town hall, with foundations dating back to Elizabethan times, served as a prison until 1830. Eight of the prison cells are still intact, the Cowbridge museum using six of them.

The main street has a number of Georgian houses, so the town has layers of historical sites and visions across the centuries.

It has retained an attraction into the modern day as a place of culture and sport in clubs and societies, the aesthetic lying alongside the athletic, with retail and leisure adding a ready lay-by for those seeking distraction or a breather away from the pace of living, ambling in shops or contemplating life in the repaste resting places, pubs and restaurants. In 2017 it was named as one of the best places in Wales to live and at the time of writing parking is always free, which is a magnet in itself.

My early connection centred on the school, Cowbridge Grammar School for Boys. Founded in 1608, it had close links with Jesus College, Oxford. It was a kind of psuedo public school in part, in that it accepted boarders, fifty boys from the old County of Glamorgan being offered places there. I was there for just two terms, but it left an indelible impression upon me, unlike Sir Anthony Hopkins apparently, who also went there as a pupil and, if reports are true, didn't much care for it. The building itself was old and drafty, with brain-boxed tradition and physical discomfort fighting for prominence. Very often, though, the lifeblood of any building or place is the people who roam its confines.

The school had a staffroom of characters. The headteacher was Idwal Rees, a classics man from Swansea who had played in the Welsh rugby international side that beat the New Zealand All Blacks in 1935, 13-12. A big victory. The captain that day was the cast iron centre three-quarter Claude Davely, and the team included such men as Wolf Wooller, Haydn Tanner, Cliff Jones and the redoubtable Idwal Rees. Allegedly, the celebrations included a giant gorgonzola cheese being stuck fast to the dining room wall of the Queen's Hotel, Cardiff.

Idwal, as headteacher, was a disciplinarian. If needs required it, in flashing his cane. Idwal would have made d'Artagnan of The Three Musketeers with his rapier, come a far-off second best, both in style and effect. Sometimes in morning assembly he announced arrangements for buses in the afternoon for the boys travelling in from surrounding areas. Some mornings, because there were so many boys named Jones, Williams, Evans or other Welsh names, Latin flair took over.

'Jones septem St Nicholas, bus novem, Jones octo Llanmaes, bus undecim, Jenkins triginta Pontyclun, also on bus octo. Jenkins, if you don't know what bus that is, ask Jones octo Llanmaes, he's on the same one.' The Latin quoted here is there or thereabouts. It was all quite a few years ago.

The boarding masters were almost artistic in balance and loco parentis responsibility. One was Wyn Oliver, the

PE master, a bachelor who stood five foot five inches when he was feeling well but was a hand grenade of explosive energy, an elusive and fast rugby winger and a sprinter for Wales in the 1958 British Empire and Commonwealth Games in Cardiff. The other was Iolo Davies, also a bachelor and Classics man, intellectual and academic, from his wayward hair to his untied shoelaces. He was the Mr Chips of Cowbridge Grammar School, offering an alternative society, a parallel school world where all the boys had a right to be. Their study was an architectural showpiece in its extreme informality, stacked to the ceiling with shelves of books, a gap here and there allowing a half-drunk whisky bottle to titillate and tempt. Iolo's cavalry twill trouser legs were in no danger of being mud-splattered, ending as they did some six inches from shoe and pavement.

Iolo's dedication to the school was way beyond accepted duty. His mode of transport was a minibus, so that it could be of use for the boys. He turned out a weekly newspaper called *The Lion* and the school magazine, *The Bovian*, was released every term. He also wrote a book called *A Certaine Schoole*, a comprehensive history of Cowbridge Grammar School. He eventually became the headteacher, but after comprehensive education was brought in Iolo became disenchanted, gave it all up and, for a while, went to work on the narrow-gauge Talyllyn Railway.

The two boarding masters were good to me. After a particularly heavy night researching the watering holes of the town they would always suggest that I sleep the night in a spare room next to the boarders dormitories to avoid the walk home to Crossways on the far hill.

So many influential characters I could mention: Darwin Adams, who, during his maths lessons, would sometimes come and sit in 'his chair' in the staffroom. It was his chair because, from it, he had a good view through the window into the classroom and he could check what the class was doing, while he had a puff on his pipe.

Sid Harris, another Classics man, with a hard, physical, successful sporting past as a centre three-quarter for the All Whites, Swansea RFC. Yet, he oozed common sense and a back-boned morality. I can see him now, on St David's Day, when we had the afternoon off, standing on a red post box at the edge of town with a daffodil in his mouth, having told the sixth form boys, 'Now, listen to me, the staff are drinking in the Horse and Groom this afternoon, alright, I don't want to see any of you near there.' That allowed them to graze in the Bear Hotel, the Edmundes Arms, the Duke of Wellington or the Vale of Glamorgan undisturbed.

He also related a lovely tale of morality and decorum about courting his wife. 'She was a nurse,' he said, 'and one night I was late taking her back to the nurses' home. It was locked, so we walked around the building and came across a window that was lightly open. I climbed up, prized it open further, and I then helped her to climb in. In doing so, I inadvertently put both my hands on her backside, palm to cheek, and heaved. Well, boys, I felt, in that moment, that I was committed. In the morning I did the honourable thing, I asked her to marry me.'

Finally, my respect for Jeff Alden. He was my geography

head of of department. What a lovely man, a gentleman in every way. In later years he was to become Head of Sixth Form and, at A Level results time, the number of students who didn't quite get the required grade whom he managed to 'talk' the university authorities into granting acceptance is beyond measure. When he retired he turned to his other love, history, producing books and a DVD of the town. He died far too young. The Town Hall has now a local history studies room, the Jeff Alden Room, in his honour. Rightly so, say I.

So, a small patch on the quilt that is Wales with so many tales. Llantwit Major, Llandow and Cowbridge, all close together. Many can be recalled in annals, because they are what this area was, is and will become. Some tales, though, are trapped in a drawer cabinet in the mind, ready for release at a personal level, the recall, the return, when musing on events as they effected you; general, accepted facts, uncertain fiction or fancy perhaps, but all with a clarity that you know, for certain, you were sculpted, moulded and forever changed by the experience of just passing through.

12. Owain Glyndŵr and Me

Carmarthenshire

One moment she was there, running, seeking, sniffing excitedly as dogs do... Then she was gone, as in a puff of wind, had there been a breeze at all. Becky had disappeared, without trace and without a clue.

It was on Maerdy Mountain, not far from the Darren and the glacial ridge that looks down on Cwmdare. Frantic searches and calls were to no avail. The only solution seemed to point to the irregular and uncertain moorland sweep and the many sink holes dotted along the ridge-top terrain. Becky had fallen into one of the holes.

After panic came organisation and a plan. Down in the Cynon Valley volunteers were gathered and a search party formed. They were made up of professionals and ardent amateurs. I was once told that professionals should always take the lead, but amateurs, especially those with local or specialised knowledge, had their valued place. 'Don't underestimate amateurs, Roy, ever,' was the advice given to me by a man with a coal-sack full of common sense at the ready in any crisis or task. 'Remember now, professionals built the Titanic, but it was an amateur who built the Ark...and I know which queue I would have been in for a ticket.'

As the search group set off, it was then that the dog joined them. Everyone there thought it was somebody else's dog, so no one took a great deal of notice. After climbing to the top of the ridge the dog moved to the front of the pack and stayed there, weaving every which way in finding a sheep trail or safe ground for treading. Without thinking, the pack of volunteers seemed to follow his lead. There was a kind of directness in this dog's mental map.

No one questioned its orienteering because they had no idea where to start looking for Becky anyway.

The dog suddenly stopped mid-march, looking downward. There was no yelping, barking or wagging of an excited tail, just a downward stare. Then, in the stillness, there was barking from a distance, not from across the moorland and a far-off place but deep down in the earth, somewhere below the crack and hole that the dog had found. Shouts of 'Becky' from the group of volunteers drew answering yelps. Becky was down there.

Careful digging and clearing, the dropping of ropes and a slow descent by one volunteer was, with effort, successful. Becky was nearly 100 feet down, cold and frightened, but applause broke out as she was quietly pulled to the surface. Gathering their equipment, they closed as a group and began the journey back. Where had the 'guide dog' gone, the one that had suddenly appeared to lead them? Nowhere to be seen. They looked at each other quizzically, but there was no answer to the raised eyebrows. Their four-legged guide was gone, as silently and unexpectedly as it had joined them. Complete mystery.

That incident reminded me of an adventure we had as boys on the Black Mountain. Berian and I had set out with our dandelion and burdock pop and condensed milk sandwiches on a hike over the ridge between Brynaman and the north-facing slope, looking down at Gwynfe, the road to Llangadog and the rolling hills of enclosed fields stretching away towards rural Mid Wales.

We stopped and rested, ready for our vittles, against a big bluish-grey boulder, one of the thousands carried there by the last ice sheet to give the mountain its name. We were just in mid-picnic when it happened – I bit my lip in fright as a man suddenly popped his head above the boulder.

'Good morning boys, fine day for it.' He was beautifully dressed, as I remember, like one of those hikers you saw in magazines advertising walks in Switzerland, but he didn't have a hat with a feather in it, nor did his trousers end at the knee with long thick socks going south from there.

He had a round, friendly face, was very convivial, jovial in fact, and, thinking back, he was wearing a waistcoat, a tie, and a jacket I recognised years later as Harris Tweed. His only yield to the moorland terrain was a pair of boots and he did carry a stick. Neither Berian nor I could understand where he came from. When he finally bid us farewell we allowed a few minutes to gather ourselves after the shock of his appearance and then we popped up to scan a stare over the boulder. No sign of him. The moorland stretched for miles. We could see the escarpment dropping down to Llyn y Fan Fach, Lady of the Lake country, way in the distance. He'd gone...disappeared. No trace.

We sat back down, unnerved for a while, and then I was distracted by the view down towards the hamlet of Gwynfe, or Capel Gwynfa as marked on maps. I knew the place well because my mother would take me to visit our relatives there two or three times a year. My great-uncle James Jones lived there, on Ysgyborwen Farm. Remarkable man, a county councilor; no car, one leg, three wives. He had lost his leg in a threshing machine accident on the farm. When his first wife fell ill, a cousin came to look after her. When she died, James thought it only right and proper to marry the cousin, lest there be talk locally that an unmarried young woman was seeing to his needs. After a while the cousin also fell ill, so another cousin came to look after her. Forming a pattern, the first cousin also died and James, true to moral code, married the second cousin-cum-nurse. Extraordinary. He didn't need to go courting, the wives came to the house like 'meals on wheels'. Number three, Great-Auntie May, did see him out, however.

There were three pubs on the road over the mountain from Brynaman to Llangadog, the New Inn, The Pont Aber and The Three Horseshoes, all three now gone, sadly. The New Inn's owner was a large lady, in body, in character and in personality. Generally known as 'Madam', she had come from the Cwmllynfell area and her lounge with no bar had a fine three-piece suite, easy chairs, ornaments on the mantelpiece and paintings on the walls. It was the first time I'd seen such a posh, 'make yourself at home' pub room looking like someone's private living room.

On the road onwards past the two other pubs, you can turn off left and head towards Bethlehem...not Bethlehem, Judea, but Bethlehem, Llangadog. It was famous at Christmastide because you could post your cards there and get your stamps franked 'Bethlehem'. Finally, and sadly,it closed and the franking machine was moved to Llandeilo, though there was a move to get it re-opened just for Christmas.

On the hill to the south of Bethlehem is Garn Goch, an Iron Age fort with massive ramparts dating from the first millennium B.C. to the invasion by the Romans. It was probably inhabited as far back as the Bronze Age, and you can walk the ridge to Y Gaer Fach and Y Gaer Fawr, taking in both the small and large forts. It was a bustling community, farming and making goods to sell and barter, but it also housed fierce warriors, defending their community against the invaders.

A number of Roman governors fought hard against the various tribes of Wales. Scapula was one, campaigning against the tribes the Romans called the Silures and Ordovices. Caradog, one of the main leaders of the Britons, escaped to join the Silures, combined forces with the Ordivices and stirred them into rebellion, so it is said. Some actually believe that Caradog resisted the Romans right there at Garn Goch.

Oddly, at a funeral in Maesteg, I was approached by someone at the 'ham on plates' post-crematorium gathering on the very subject of the Silures tribe. He suggested that Welsh historical facts should be placed on beer mats as a gesture towards lifelong learning.

'For instance,' he said, 'did you know that in the skirmishes between the Silures and the Romans, the Silures were ahead on victories but the fixture list had to be suspended when the Romans suddenly left?' To be honest I didn't know that, but the historical facts beer mat is not a bad idea.

On the road to Llangadog, instead of turning left to Bethlehem you can turn right to Llanddeusant and the back country that leads to Llyn y Fan and the tale of the Lady of the Lake. Famed in Wales, the tale is well-known of the young, vibrant farmer who was one day enchanted by a lovely lady who suddenly emerged from Llyn y Fan Fach, overlooked by the ridges of the Carmarthenshire Fans. Incidentally, there is also Llyn y Fan Fawr, a bigger lake, but it doesn't get as much good mythical press.

The farmer was besotted and plagued the lady to marry him. She, of course, relented and agreed, but on conditions. If he hit her, or touched her with iron three times, she was off back to the lake.

He had no chance. After a seemingly happy marriage blessed with three children, the three dreaded occasions came to pass: once at a wedding, once at a funeral and once at the blessing of a new-born child. On each occasion her behaviour was deemed unacceptable, like laughing with joy at the funeral. She maintained that her joy was released because the deceased was now free from all life's troubles and strife. Crying at the blessing of the child was her reaction to the child having to face all of life's burdens and problems, and the wedding scene centred on the fact that she knew that the bridegroom would soon die.

Each time, the farmer only touched her lightly to get her to control herself, but in her book that was enough. She returned to the lake, taking all his worldly goods with her. If you visit the lake these days, quietly walk around the water's edge seeking the mark the plough made as it was pulled towards and then beneath the water. Also notice that few birds appear to sing there. The pragmatist and cynic will tell you that very few trees grow on that moorland setting, so the birds have nowhere to land and don't bother to visit. No myth there then.

Some believe that if, in fact, the farmer touched his wife

with metal, a horseshoe, a ring and a bridle respectively, then the story might come from a time when Stone Age people met Iron Age tribes with their swords and jewellery.

Whatever the base of the story there is a strong generational heritage, for their children, allegedly, became the famed Physicians of Myddfai. Bestowed upon them was the gift of healing and, in fact, this area of Wales could be the birthplace of modern medicine. The village of Myddfai is close at hand, near Llandovery. Their herbal remedies and lists of medicinal compounds can be found in many books, notably at the National Botanic Garden in the Towy Valley.

Llangadog itself is an ancient place of interest, situated between Llandovery and Llandeilo. It used to be far more bustling than it is now, with a large saw mill, a production centre for huge concrete pipes and a successful creamery, the butter produced being used by British Airways. The Central Wales Railway line also has a station there.

For its size, there are quite a few refreshing watering holes, The Red Lion being one. It is listed as a coaching inn, re-built in 1839-40, possibly using stones from the demolished Danyrallt Mansion.

Rumour has it that during the Rebecca Riots, when men dressed as women attacked toll gates in the area, some of the planning was done in this inn.

Following the A40 towards Llandeilo, a stop at Llanwrda is a must. No one knows where Owain Glyndŵr is buried, and many maintain that the myth and mystery must be maintained. Was Owain buried just across the border in England? His daughter, Alys, married Sir John Scudamore of Herefordshire and it is rumoured that Owain was hidden on their estate at the old manorial seat at Mornington Straddle, near Kentchurch. There is an overgrown mound there in which it is rumoured Owain rests. The family and others ignored ransoms to reveal his last resting place and Owain, it is said, was disguised as a family chaplain and tutor for a time.

Or was Owain buried in Llanwrda after his days, if only for a short while? A story by Alex Gibbon strongly suggests that he was moved from Mornington Straddle and buried under the altar of St Cawrdaf Church, Llanwrda. In these days of DNA, there must be a way of checking. It is only a small church, but what a big story, and an even bigger question.

Llanwrda is also on the junction of the A482 from Lampeter as it joins the A40. Along that road lies the track of my heritage, at least on my mother's side, twisting and turning over the River Dulais seven times in a couple of miles as you head for Pumsaint, Crugybar, Caio and the Dolau Cothi Roman gold mines.

I once spent the night in the Dolau Cothi Inn, Pumsaint, in a back bedroom. I opened the curtains and still remember the sheer blackness of the sky and the canopy of wondrous stars, the Milky Way shimmering through the centre of the heavens. My two great-aunties lived in Caio, my homeland, Hannah and Marged. They were sisters but hadn't spoken for years, so when we visited we had lunch with Hannah and her husband Dafydd. The house was pristine, just off the road to the village. Hannah had been a teacher and Dafydd kept bees. Marged was a different kettle of fish. As we arrived in her cottage, the first thing she always asked, in Welsh, was, 'Shwd ma hi lawr na?' 'How is she down there? Alright, is she?'

Marged was interested in politics and the ways of the world, but not house cleaning; you could find magazines behind her cushion dated 1932. How I loved tea-time in her house though, homely, no fuss, lovely bread and butter and jam. She was married to Dafydd too, another Dafydd, more rough and ready than the first. She lived in Brunant Cottage, next door to the Brunant Arms. I remember my father going in there for a pint and being charged one shilling and sixpence; it was one shilling and twopence in Brynaman. After a while the landlord realised he was related to Marged and said, 'You belonging to Marged, are you? Oh, there's fourpence back, I thought you were a tourist.'

I broke the record in Caio for not going to the toilet. It was a bucket out the back, hanging over a stream if you could manage the angle, as the village was not on the main drains. I went twelve hours on a 'no-go' stint.

Now the thing is, as to heritage, I have a frustration. I don't know who my grandfather was, nor my great-grandfather. I was told my great-grandmother had my grandmother when she was twelve, the age of consent in Carmarthenshire then being thirteen.

The dilemma centres on the lost men in my maternal lineage. Now, my great-grandmother and my grandmother worked as servants in grand houses or estates in the Llandeilo area. Were these missing, guilty men other servants? Or were they, more probably, the masters of the house?

Do you know, if I could only prove it, I probably own most of east Carmarthenshire. Now, that's another DNA test to consider. Owain Glyndŵr, and then me.

13. Outpatients in Patrishow

South Powys

'Going private'. When did that habit and procedure come in, then? How soon after the formation of the NHS did the move to get specialist help turn to 'going private'? Paying for treatment, ensuring fast response, seeking out the best in the 'get you better faster' business and jumping the queue. Most people go down that trail if needs must these days, but, decades ago, it was a big social leap. Some were chesty and showy about it and didn't mind who knew, because it was a mark of status I suppose, but others kept a low profile, out of embarrassment or a disturbing thought that they were being disloyal to 'the system'.

Nowadays, of course, that road to 'select' treatment has opened up to a network of routes, some staying on the medical, others seeking out alternatives. Some go modern and homeopathic, others return to the ways of ancient wisdom or even to the spiritual.

Some of the 'old ways' are mentioned in another chapter of this book: goose grease covered by a woman's nylon stocking as a cure for a sore throat, the white skin inside an egg-shell on a boil to draw an infection out, dock leaves after being stung by nettles, and rubbing raw steak or bacon on a wart and burying it in the garden, so that in withering in the soil and decaying the wart drops off as well. I could add dropping cold keys down your back to stop a nosebleed, or tying one end of a piece of string around a rotten tooth and the other around a doorknob, standing on one side of the door to wait for someone to suddenly yank the door open from the other side. Drastic, but effective on occasions.

The ancient ways take us back, in some instances, to

the Physicians of Myddfai. For a burn, take fern roots and pound well with butter, apply in a plaster to the injury, it will remove the ardent pain. Even when I was young butter was suggested for a burn. Was that really wise, butter on a burn?

Other remedies from the Myddfai Medical School included: For a bleeding nose, take a nettle, pound it well and then stick it up your nose. For a thorn wound, take lard, the roots of nettles (nettles again, they appear to be a good standby), pound them well, apply to the wound nine times. With God's help a cure will set in. Unless the Good Lord is working a three-day week, of course. For a bigger problem, diarrhea, take seven eggs, twice as much of clarified honey, a portion of wheaten loaf reduced to crumbs and a pennyworth of powdered pepper...boil them up and consume them warm. Don't drink for as long as you can. I don't know about that, when does dehydration come in there?

For the Myddfai men, the three stable medicines were water, honey and labour. Some people went for alcoholic spirits to help boost the metabolism, though it happened in reverse for my mother. When I was young, we were sleeping in my *Mamgu's* house one night because my mother was helping my grandmother to tend to Dick, a sick lodger and by then one of the family. He was in the back bedroom, in dire straits, sadly. I was sleeping between my two bachelor uncles in the front bedroom, down in the valley of the feather mattress, when my mother dramatically came into the room. 'Dick is dead!' she said. 'He suddenly sat up in bed and asked for a brandy. I gave him one, he swigged it down and collapsed back on the bed...dead. I think I've killed him!'

For some, one attractive treatment, especially for the pure of heart or the desperate of mind, is the healer, either by prayer, touch, or the hidden force of nature.

I have been told tales of success from healers but I have also learnt of arrests being made because of an over-zealous 'laying on of hands'. As for nature, it has no hidden agenda. If there is a power for healing in certain spots on the planet, it's all to the good. 'There is more to heaven and Earth, Horatio. Than are dreamt of in your philosophy.' So said old Will Shakespeare, and I have an entirely open mind on such matters.

I do know of one healing place: Partrishow. I cannot argue with some of the positive reports. It lies on the southern edge of the Black Mountains, in the Grwyne Fawr Valley. The river is a tributary of the Usk, joining its flow at Glangrwyney west of Abergavenny. You cross over it on the A40. The Grwyne Fawr Valley was the site of the murder of the Norman Marcher Lord Richard de Clare by the Welsh under Iorwerth ab Owain and his brother in 1136. The incident caused more than a little bother and skirmishes and conflict ensued for quite a while as a result.

On a geological level, there is the presence of a weakness known as the Neath disturbance in the area, although, knowing many people in Neath as I do, they would rightly deny any responsibility.

Partrishow is tucked away above Forest Coal Pit, about five miles from Abergavenny, but I tend to approach it on the minor road that heads into the back hills from the small but lovely market town of Crickhowell.

There has been a settlement there at least since the Iron Age. Crug Howell, from which the town gets is name, is also called Table Mountain because of its flat top. It overlooks the town and the entire summit is taken up by an Iron Age Celtic hillfort with its clearly visible earth and stone ditch and rampart.

The Normans also set up a base here at the motte-and-bailey castle, the remains of which still exist on the edge of town.

A well-know and quirky feature of Crickhowell is the bridge spanning the River Usk. Built in 1706 and modified in 1828-30, the bridge has thirteen arches on the upstream side but only twelve on the downstream side. Drinkers leaving the Bridge Inn could spend many an ale-fuelled late afternoon or evening working out the mathematics of that conundrum. There is a reason and solution. Ask a local.

Across the bridge lies the village of Llangattock, below the high limestone ridge that separates the Usk Valley from the old industrial valleys of south-east Wales. It is a place I know well, for I was happily the headteacher of the school for a few years. It is an attractive place, with the Monmouthshire and Brecon canal cutting east to west on the slope that leads to the high ridge and the road to Ebbw Vale.

It was just below that ridge I ran into a 'war game' late one evening as I returned from a governors' meeting at the school. The Falklands War had just kicked off and troops were training on the moorlands. Innocently, I drove straight into army vehicles, a helicopter dropping troops, men running everywhere and two Landrovers with flags that appeared to be the HQ for the judges and arbitrators deciding who was dead, injured or captured. It was all quite exciting and exhilarating until an officer ran over to me and loudly questioned my presence, my purpose and my parentage. I got to the Yellow Brick Road, the A465 Heads of the Valleys expressway to the Milky Way, totally bemused as to whether I had been declared a casualty, a spy, an insurgent or just a local yokel.

Llangattock has a compendium of stories in its own right, including ghosts and superstitions. Children there picked up directives from the older generations like, 'Whoever breaks a wren's nest shall never know heavenly rest' and, 'I've lived too near the wood to be frightened by the owls.' The behaviour of birds and animals was said to have some influence on the lives of human beings.

On the ghost scene, there is the tale of a farm labourer returning to one of the farms between Llangattock and Llangynidr along a snow-filled lane on the south side of the River Usk when he saw a funeral procession approaching. He stepped aside, but as they passed he saw that they were not treading on the road but on air, their feet level with the snowy hedge. A few days later, after heavy snow, there was a real funeral and such was the depth of snow that the whole cortege had to make its way at hedgerow height.

There are so many other tales from the area, like the field above the hillside bank of the canal that is known as the Devil's Ridge, Cae Cefn Cythraul. Why? Ah, well, those tales are for another chapter, or possibly another book.

Back now across the bridge to Crickhowell and another historic feature is The Bear Hotel, a former coaching inn that has retained its post-horses archway and original cobbles to this day.

The town has also made its mark on the world with its famous sons, including Admiral Sir Walter Cowan, or Tich Cowan, who became a Royal Navy Admiral serving in both World War I and World War II. In the latter he was one of the oldest British servicemen on active duty. Another Crickhowell-born world traveller in the military was Colonel Sir George Everest. A surveyor and geographer, he became the Surveyor General of India and, in 1856, gave his name to the world's highest mountain, no doubt having uttered the exclamation 'Will you look at the size of that!' on discovering it. His family lived for a while in the house that is now The Manor Hotel on the edge of town, looking down on a beautiful stretch of the Usk Valley.

So, at last, to climb the hill. On the minor road that heads out of Crickhowell into the back country south of the Black Mountains, we head for Partrishow. The road is very rural and narrow in places, and care has to be taken to seek out the signs.

In Wales there are lots of places where you can go back, back to the mists of different times. Wales is a small place, so it doesn't take long to go over the hill and far away. In some places the past is so present that it sends a shiver down your spine. There are hills here, some gentle, some higher, like the Sugar Loaf to the south and the Black Mountains edging nearer from the north. When I finally find Patrishow Church, the spot is beautiful in its setting.

The serenity is sacred and the quietness almost loud in its intensity. The church itself is small, above a hollow and not at all flamboyant; it seems to know its place in its tranquil haven. The pace of life is measured here in small steps.

Despite the quiet, the area is somehow potent and there is a touch of the dramatic, for, on opening the door, you soon see the painted image of a man, clearly visible through the lime treatment on the back wall. He is a skeleton, carrying a spade, what appears to be an axe and an hourglass. Apparently, it is an eerie reminder of the mortality of man with time running out. A figure of doom. However number of times they lime the wall, the image will have its say and seep through. It was painted in the seventeenth century by a man who made a living painting pub signs, so the sacred and the spirits were all the same to him. There are other paintings on the church walls too, I have to say.

When I visited I met the self-taught organist, Denver Green, a remarkable man. I asked him what size of congregation they got most Sundays. 'Forty on a good Sunday, sixteen on a poor one,' was his reply. He did admit that in his time there the service had sometimes started with no one there, but the Rector carried on regardless... People would come, invariably, answering the call no doubt.

A more joyous and uplifting image in the church is the exquisite rood screen, carved out of Irish oak. At the rear of the church is an unusual parish chest carved out of a solid tree trunk with iron bands around it and three locks, once used for the safe keeping of parish valuables.

St Issui, a hermit and healer, lived here long ago. His special place was down in the hollow, near where the road takes a sharp turn. The story goes that St Issui was murdered and a traveller, on hearing this, recalled with gratitude his treatment by Issui when he suffered from leprosy. He returned with a sack full of gold so that a church could be built. In that hollow below the church we come to the special place of well-being this is St Issui's Well. It is only yards from the road and if you follow the stream you will see trees where tokens and coins have been pressed into their trunks and ribbons been tied to the branches.

The well itself is not what you would probably have in mind as an image. It is not the shape of a well, but more of a small, trapped pool contained within a very small space. The water is not deep, in fact, after a dry spell the bottom is lined with mud and can be said to be unimpressive. Yet, if tales are to be believed, that small contained well of water has a power. It is for bathing, not for drinking, so I'm told.

I once spoke to a lady who told me her experience of being cured. She had an operation on her foot and things had gone terribly wrong. Within a few months she had it confirmed by medical specialists that there was no cure and that the original problem with her foot would continue to deteriorate until she was unable to walk.

Someone told her of St Issui's Well and, in desperation, she visited the place. She walked with extreme difficulty to the awkward spot where the well was situated and quietly dipped her foot into the water. Although a committed Christian, she did not pray. She did, however, experience a feeling of joy and well-being. When she got back to the road she suddenly wondered how she had made the walk so easily.

A few weeks later she visited the medical specialist for a planned examination. He was amazed. 'What has been happening here?' he queried. 'There is no sign that there has been anything wrong with your foot.' When she asked the specialist what he had written on his report, he told her 'miraculous cure'.

I have spoken to quite a few people who have had wonderfully similar experiences in other holy places and I take it entirely at face value. My mind is completely open on such matters. Whether a physical ailment is cured by powerful, unseen properties or elements within nature, or whether, psychologically, it is a sudden surge in the mind that positively affects the body, or whether it is something else on an astral, spiritual plane doesn't really matter. As long as it works. Really works. Just accept it as a gift.

I have to say I have re-visited the well and, just to test the water, dipped in my fingers, just to see if my creeping arthritis could be addressed and neutered. I have to report no real improvement…but it could be that without the quick dip the digits would have been far worse by now. Perhaps my problem wasn't serious enough anyway.

It is a special place, you can feel it. I'll visit again…for a second opinion.

14. Pooh Sticks to Pontypool

Torfaen

It was in September of 1961 that I first came across it. In the first week of my student days I was just coming out of Astey's Cafe, on the corner at the Central Bus Station, Cardiff, where I'd partaken of another 'first', a Clark's pie. There it was, on the destination board of a bus leaving the station: British.

Now, my subject was geography, but I'd never come across that place name before. Was it in Wales, I wondered? Indeed it was, because fate decreed that the name came up in my college course a few months later. As spring lengthened the days, we were asked to undertake a geographical survey of two places...Aberthaw, on the Vale of Glamorgan coast, and British in the Afon Lwyd Valley above Abersychan, just north of Pontypool. Incredibly, as life unfolded, I was to return many years later to speak at the awards night in Abersychan Secondary School.

I have a photograph of myself and a fellow student, Thomas Gilmor Nimrod Jones, of Saron, 'Spots' to his friends, for reasons unknown, unless he'd had a difficult facial problem at the explosion of puberty. For some reason we are seen shaking hands in the photograph, standing on the platform of Abersychan Station. The relief road from Blaenavon south to Pontypool was built on that closed railway line some years ago.

I was always uncertain about surveys. There is a line that crosses from information to imposition, or even impertinence. In the sixth form of Amman Valley Grammar School, Ammanford, we had also been asked to undertake a survey in the geography class. It was on land usage in semi-rural areas within our locality. Questions to farmers about the number of acres they had and how many sheep grazed on them were usually met with a stony stare and a curt 'Who wants to know?' After a few visits, news got about that we might be fifth columnists for the Tax Office, our youthful faces being merely a clever Revenue ruse, so our survey forms were left with massive gaps. We changed to a transport survey in the end.

Gilmor and I vowed that our British and Aberthaw surveys would be sensitively made; rather than cause offence, we resorted to guesswork and fiction. Well, it was only for our coursework, surely no one would seek out the absolute gospel in council records.

British, in fact, was intriguing. It had very salubrious, notable London connections and was named after an iron works built there in 1825 by the British Iron Company. The community consisted of just a very few short terraced streets on the valley side above Abersychan and one access to it was through an industrial arch called the Big Arch, because it was...and still is. The terraced houses were carbon copies of so many others in The Valleys. The ribbon developments were one and the same.

They reminded me of my own terraced street in Brynaman. It was a street on which I had eight aunties, none of whom were related to me, just surrogate aunties because we lived that close. So close, in fact, that you could hear someone change their mind from four doors away. There weren't many secrets in those days. Our toilets were 'out the back', semi-detached, with a one-brick thickness between the two comfort corners. In effect we were sitting just a couple of feet away from either Rhys or Catura Price, our 'attached by toilets' neighbours, and a cordial 'good morning' was tempting, if not a prolonged conversation on the news of the day. Toilet paper was the local newspaper...the posh people cut it into squares. Proper toilet paper didn't get to the village until the early '50s. Our 'en-suite' bathroom, or aluminium bath, if you like, hung on a nail by the back door, to be used daily by colliers returning from work and for the rest of the family on Fridays or Sundays, depending on family habit, British was probably of similar vintage and design.

The development of the iron works and the community had an office building and an area known as The Quadrangle, both designed by the architect Decimus Burton, who also designed London Zoo and Hyde Park. So, definitely a salubrious London connection, but quite a few decades behind in toilet design from the grand city.

As with so many industrial areas of the valleys of south Wales, that area has been derelict for many years. In fact, it is the largest remaining site of industrial dereliction in south-east Wales and there are plans to develop the 1300-acre brown field iron works site Navigation colliery, using, in part, open-cast mining over a section the size of forty rugby pitches.

I must report that the survey of the area by Thomas Gilmor Nimrod Jones and myself attained a good mark. Not quite gold star level, but sufficiently high to be very acceptable without being too showy and certainly effective in leaving Abersychan and British with a warm spot in my memory bank.

North of Abersychan, the road takes you through a

lovely wooded and rural section of Afan Lwyd, onwards to Blaenavon, which left a searing mark on Welsh industrial history. It remains high profile on the heritage and tourist trail today. Out of a 2000 site list it is firmly one of the most important on the European Industrial Heritage Trail. Big Pit remains a massive attraction and if the volunteer-run railway line nearby could stretch just one station further north than its current last stop, then it would qualify as the highest station on normal gauge lines in the whole of Britain. So I was told, and I am prepared to go along with the notion and the enthusiasm.

In the centre of the upper valley, Blaenavon Iron Works is such an important place in terms of what made Wales, who made Wales and, during the industrialisation of The Valleys, where Wales was. If you stand there in the quiet of the modern-day scene, you cannot help but be affected by a sense of place, when thoughts fill your mind of the sheer vigour and burning atmosphere that reverberated in the production of iron and the lives of the people who moulded their existence around it. The Blaenavon Hall is a magnificent edifice and evidence of how, beyond the sheer toil and effort, culture, the arts, education and personal development were driven forward to fulfil so many inner needs and callings.

Blaenavon is a special place, *Rape of the Fair Country* land. The moorland beyond the town stretches in pock-marked spoil heaps and a barren treeless landscape towards Brynmawr and the Clydach Gorge, dropping down from Llanelli Hill to Gilwern and the Monmouthshire-Brecon Canal as it heads on a slow curve back south to Pontypool and, in its day, Newport.

Rape of the Fair Country was written by Alexander Cordell and first published in 1959 after the author moved to and fell in love with this area. It eased into his soul. His novels follow in part the life of Iestyn Mortymer, in work, in family, in love and in insurrection, taking us through the Klondike and melting pot that was this vast patch on the Welsh historical quilt at a time of growing tension between ironmaster and the new trade unionists. Cordell had an affinity with two peoples in his life, the Chinese and the Welsh; both became a part of his psyche and passion.

Returning to Abersychan through the narrow section of the valley, along the Afon Lwyd where the current could race 'Pooh-sticks' the speed of a car when in full-flow, we head south to Pontypool and the many chapters it adds to the saga. There are two Pontypools, of course, one being in Ontario, Canada. That village took a leap forward when the Canadian Pacific Railway, west to east, laid a track through it on a direct line to Toronto, but further prominence and profile came when Pontypool was the given name of a horror film, based on a book written by Tony Burgess entitled *Pontypool Changes Everything*. I don't know if it did anything for the tourist trade of that Pontypool.

Our own Pontypool, on the other hand, is extreme-horror-free and has a notable history as one of the earliest industrial towns in Wales. Its links to the iron industry date back to the early fifteenth century and, later, there was an abundance of resources in the Afon Lwyd Valley for the manufacturing of iron, coal, iron ore, charcoal and water power. Blast furnaces were developed at a rate and from the mid-eighteenth century, as the Industrial Revolution took hold, there was massive expansion in south Wales. Pontypool had to compete with other important centres in The Valleys like Merthyr Tydfil, Tredegar and Blaenavon, but it retained a niche, specialising in tinplate. Tram roads and canals were built to accommodate the transport requirements.

The importance of Pontypool in the heyday of world iron and coal production is without question, but as the years roll towards new centuries, what is it that grabs the attention and interest of the passing stranger or the casual visitor?

Well, Pontypool Park leaps out as a candidate to impress any traveller. It was the historic seat of the Hanbury family, influential entrepreneurs in the industrial maelstrom. To this day it is a beautiful and extensive park and the playing venue of the famed Pontypool Rugby Club.

I once suggested a competition on BBC Radio Wales to pinpoint the most attractive rugby ground in the whole of Wales. As I remember, Pontypool was edged out into second place by Aberaeron rugby ground in the far west, where the field looks across Cardigan Bay to the Llŷn Peninsula in the far north. Abertillery did quite well too, and one or two clubs did complain that they had not been visited by the judges at all. Others protested that the hospitality in other clubs had been somewhat too lavish and could only have been prepared to doctor the judgement of those in charge of the marks, given out of a hundred.

In the Park, as well as various leisure and sporting facilities, there is a dry ski slope, well hidden by the trees on the sloping valley side. The Folly Tower is also nearby, located within the grounds of a working farm, octagonal in shape and roughly forty feet (twelve metres) high. The actual date of construction is unknown, but it is thought to have been around 1765 to 1770, commissioned by John Hanbury, the local landowner and ironmaster who owned the Park. There is reference that the elevated spot on which the tower stands, some 1000 feet (305 metres), was formerly a Roman watchtower. Allegedly, nearly 20,000 people gathered there in May 1935 to celebrate the Silver Jubilee of King George V.

It began to fall into disrepair and in 1937 Myfanwy Haycock, the local illustrator and poet, penned the following verse:

Here where the hill holds heaven in her hands
High above Monmouthshire the grey tower stands,
He is weather-worn and scarred, and very wise,
For rainbows, clouds and stars shine through your eyes.

In 1940 the War Office ordered that it be demolished, lest it become a landmark for the Lufwaffe in a possible attack on the Royal Ordnance Factory at ROF Glascoed. Attempts at rebuilding it were sporadic, stretching from 1946 to 1948 to 1990, when finance was secured and it finally reached for the skies, with the help of 175 tonnes of dressed stone from the recently demolished Cwmffrwdwr Primary School. It was officially opened, at last, by the Prince of Wales in July 1994.

Another secret, known, of course, to Pontypool people,

is the Shell Grotto, standing on the same ridge as the Folly Tower and 700 feet above sea level. Grottos were fashionable in the eighteenth century and were built to stimulate the deepest emotions. They suggested mysterious journeys into the earth where shadow and gloom were relieved by sparkle and, sometimes, sea shells, to lift the spirit and enhance and lighten the soul's darker recesses.

This cylindrical grotto, quite plain on the outside, giving no clue to its magical interior, is considered to be the best surviving grotto in Wales. Built, like the Folly Tower, by the Hanbury family as a summerhouse-cum-hunting lodge around the middle of the eighteenth century, it is fan vaulted. The six fans rise from six pillars, with artificial stalactites hanging from the ceiling. The ceiling, indeed, is the glory of the Grotto, covered with thousands of shells interspersed with minerals and real stalactites removed from local caves. The bones and teeth of animals are set into the floor in patterns, forming circles, stars, hearts and diamonds.

After John Hanbury died, his son, Capel Hanbury Leigh, carried on the improvements to the main house, the Park and the Grotto. The design of shells could be attributed to Capel's wife, Molly, a wealthy widow from the Knoll, in Neath. Knoll Park also had a grotto, which was largely destroyed and covered by a landslip but rediscovered many years later. The Shell Grotto also fell into disrepair, but was eventually refurbished following local commitment and financial grant aid. The route to the Grotto is a testing climb and it would always be a good idea to enquire of the council as to whether it is open. It's all very well being intrepid, but if your goal has a lock on it, disappointment can cut deep.

Down from the ridge of the Tower and the Grotto, the Park levels off into the field of dreams, the Pontypool Rugby Club rugby pitch. Looking across from the grandstand, it is a vista of green slopes and treescapes. What a coliseum it was in the 1970s, when Pontypool RFC was a fortress and some of their gladiators were known worldwide. Their prowess and the conveyor belt production of rugby forwards kept trundling towards its peak in 1983, when five of the Welsh team's forwards came from the Pontypool club.

History runs deep, for the club was a founder member of the Welsh Rugby Union in 1881, but their juggernaut front row attained stardust status during that 1970s period. The famed line-up of Bobby Windsor, Charlie Faulkner and Graham Price probably knocked the renowned Three Musketeers, The Three Amigos, the Three Tenors and the Bee Gees into a cocked hat. They were second division in profile to the steel wall who were eulogised in poetic and vibrant song by Max Boyce: 'Up and under here we go, are we ready, yes or no, up and under here we go, it's the song of the Pontypool front row.'

I once attended a rugby dinner in Llandovery RFC. The main speaker was a man mountain of a Scotsman, Gordon Brown, the famous 'Broon from Troon'. He was a lovely man who looked magnificent in his kilt and Scottish artifacts and, tragically, died far too young. In his speech, he spoke of that Pontypool front row. He was a lock forward in the second row in the days when, if there was an injury, there were no replacements. In an international match between Scotland and Wales, the Scottish prop forward was injured and had to leave the field. Gordon Brown had to move from the position of lock forward to prop, directly facing and embracing the formidable Pontypool players. In the first scrum, as they prepared to go down and engage in contact, Brown recalled how Bobby Windsor looked him in the eye and said, 'Now, Gordon, be a good boy and just quietly lean...and nothing will happen to you!'

Pontypool, what flag flyers for Welsh rugby they were. The jealous would try to decry their fame and efficiency by suggesting that they were a ten-man team, eight forwards and two half-backs, stating that the other backs could have suffered from hyperthermia in winter by getting no action or possession at all. It was even suggested that Shergar, the famous kidnapped, racehorse, could have played on the wing with Lord Lucan on his back and no one would have noticed. Not so, not so, they were a steamroller of glorious intent. It is sad to see Pontypool playing at a lower level these days, in the new organisation of rugby in Wales, but it has happened to so many clubs, especially in The Valleys. They were the glowing embers mid-week who fired the kilns at weekends, facing opposition with their locality's fire, will and commitment.

Pontypool, so much to unravel in its history and place. Just below the town, the Canal Basin has not even been mentioned. The mystery of 'British' on the bus destination board is solved, the magical grottos and the field of dreams discovered, and yet, still, there are more stories to unfold and tales untold. They await awaking and a re-discovery, if you've a mind.

15. Lay-bys on the Asphalt Artery

The A470 – Ponty to Merthyr Tydfil

Just south of Merthyr Tydfil, there is a lay-by. If you pull in there, you are in the middle of what was the tragic and massive coal tip collapse of 1966 that engulfed Pantglas School and a number of houses in Aberfan. Few people realise on their journey that the route of the A470 dual carriageway between Merthyr Tydfil and Abercynon cuts right through the track of where that deadly avalanche gathered momentum. Subsidence is too innocuous a word to describe the violence of that day. Tips four, five and seven of the black spoil heaps on the valley ridge above Merthyr Vale had been strewn on mountain streams and water courses and that scandalous negligence cost a village its children.

If you are travelling south on that section of road and stop at the lay-by, then, especially in winter when the foliage is sparse, you can look down on Aberfan Community Centre, built across the road from where Pantglas School stood. Aberfan remains a brave, recovering village and two places of pilgrimage are forever poignant and emotional places of calling. There is the cemetery, which is overpowering in its sadness and yet, spiritually, hugely impressive, where marble headstones have now replaced the vulnerable sandstone. On the site of Pantglas School itself there is the memorial garden, where each lawn marks the school classrooms and the central path lies on the central corridor of the school. If you can visit this sacred place without being affected emotionally, then I would go and see about it if I were you...your senses are surely frozen.

The lay-by on the A470, just short of the scarred hillside, allows you to make out the width of the slide by the reseeded grass that doesn't quite, even to this day, blend in with the rest of the natural valley side and slope.

Aberfan, in long-past history, is notable for another tragedy, one which gave Merthyr Tydfil its name. St Tydfil, or Tudful in Welsh, was allegedly martyred around about 480 A.D. Merthyr means martyr in Welsh, but if you go down the Latin route, martyr comes from *martyrium*, initially a martyr's tomb, but later merely a church dedicated to a saint. There is a St Tydfil's Church in Merthyr, but it is believed that Tydfil met her end at her religious community in the Taff River valley, not far from the community run by her sister at Hafod Tanglwstl, now known as the village of Aberfan.

Tydfil was the daughter of King Brychan, the half-Irish, half-Welsh ruler of Garth Madry, modern-day Brecon. Brychan clearly put himself about a bit in that he had four wives, several concubines, eleven sons and twenty-five daughters. Tydfil was his twenty-third daughter by his fourth wife. The off-spring were well educated and founded churches all over Wales, Cornwall and Brittany.

In his old age, Brychan decided to visit his children one last time. After visiting Tanglwstl, his third daughter, he moved on to visit Tydfil. His protecting forces were stretched and they were attacked by marauding Picts, with Tydfil becoming a victim to one of these attacks. Local legends add colour to the story, but there is evidence that she did exist and that she met with a violent end. She was buried within the church she founded and a Celtic Cross was put up in a clearing near the Taff. In the thirteenth century, the cross and wattle and daub church were replaced by a stone church dedicated to St. Tydfil the Martyr. This was, in turn, replaced in 1807 and rebuilt again in 1894. When the Norman church was demolished, a stone coffin was found, forming part of the foundations, along with two stone pillars, one of which was dedicated to King Brychan's son, Arthen, also killed in the battle. The site was probably kept sacred to the memory of Tydfil and her murdered family.

Why was Tydfil venerated as a saint? Well, her sacrifice for her faith and beliefs, turning the other cheek when faced with threat and violence and her selfless service in the cause of others, plus many more laudable and convincing attributes when the great ecclesiastical committee considered the applications, must have sealed it. Oh yes, she ticked all the boxes and then some, of that there is no doubt, and that grand saint stamping committee can be very picky.

Before continuing north on the A470 seeking intriguing and diversionary lay-bys of interest, it is worth double-checking and heading south to the town fondly known as Ponty. Others will argue that there is more than one Ponty, but Pontypool more easily slips to 'Pool' or 'Pooler'. Pontarddulais is accepted as 'Y bont', Pontardawe usually gets the full treatment. I could go on, good grief, there's a list of them, but as for the one true Ponty, well, you know where you are...Pontypridd.

It was actually *Pont ar y ty pridd*, the bridge by the earthen house. This is the spot where the world seriously meets The Valleys.

There has been a confused problem with this concept

I feel. We, who live in The Valleys, suffer from the Tongwynlais Gap syndrome. There is, in Tongwynlais, a definite gap or divide. As you travel south you can see it, a geographical gap which allows you through, custom free, to Cardiff. That gap also has, in-built, a social and psychological divide. Those who have lived in the capital city for years and those who reside in The Vale sometimes give the impression that they have the Valleys tribe sussed out; they know the personality, the mural wash that covers us all, and they have formed stereotypical images of the inhabitants, Valleys Man and Woman. To say, quietly and diplomatically, that this is wayward thought and demeaning in view, is to avoid the full furnace of response and reaction.

Pontypridd, closely tied to the coal and iron industries, was, in its early days, second to Treforest in urban settlement, a rural backwater of a few farmsteads. The Glamorganshire Canal and, later, the Taff Railway, taking iron and coal to the ports of Cardiff, Barry and Newport, changed all that.

For years, Ponty had two claims to international fame. Its railway platform at the station was thought to be the longest in the world. Yes, the longest in the world. To top that, its Old Bridge was, at one time, the longest single span bridge in the entire world when it was built by William Edwards in 1756. To be fair, before we get too chesty, it was Edwards' third attempt. Two fell down.

It was a perfect segment of a circle and notable features were, and still are, the three holes of differing diameters through each end of the bridge. Mind you, on completion, questions were raised as to the utility of the bridge, with the steepness of the design making it difficult to get a horse and cart across. Still, it was impressive, if only for locals to invite visitors to answer the question, 'How's that for a bridge, then?' In fact, Pontypridd was known as Newbridge after its construction. Still, needs must, and another new bridge, the Victoria Bridge, was built adjacent to the old one in 1857.

Let's not forget a cultural dimension for Ponty too. It was home to the birth of the National Anthem, 'Hen Wlad Fy Nhadau', with the music composed by James James, bardic name Iago ap Ieuan, and words written by poet Evan James, his father. Although strongly associated with Llantrisant, the colourful eccentric Dr William Price, who conducted and performed the first cremation in the United Kingdom, also made Pontypridd his home for years.

Turning north again, the A470 takes a breather at a roundabout near Abercynon. The quirk on this roundabout is the fact that there are two signs pointing to Abercynon West...in opposite directions. But worry not, either way will get you there.

Just a side-step and a couple of curves from the roundabout you can seek out the lost cemetery of Quakers Yard. The early name was Rhyd y Grug, or The Ford of the Rustling Waters, an easy crossing spot on the River Taff. It has an interesting religious history. During the early seventeenth century, those who 'dissented' from the King's religion were persecuted by imprisonment or death. By the middle of the seventeenth century, a dissenting group of Baptists, independents and Quakers were worshipping at nearby Berthlwyd Farm. The Quakers soon broke away to establish their own community and in 1667 they opened their own Quaker burial ground. The owner of the land, a Mary Chapman, left it to the Quakers in her will. Its extent was small and the Quakers didn't want to draw attention to it, and finding it these days is even more difficult, because a new road was built through the site.

Quakers Yard is a small place and it is worth mentioning that a small man, born there, though claimed as the 'Tylerstown Terror' from the Rhondda, made a huge, worldly mark on his chosen sport...boxing. He lost only 4 contests in 864, knocking 100 opponents out. Slightly built at just over 5'2" and only 7st. 10lbs in weight, he became Flyweight Champion of the World from 1916 to 1921. Known as 'The Ghost with a Hammer in His Hand' or 'The Mighty Atom', he was Jimmy Wilde.

Jimmy had a tragic end. He was mugged on Cardiff Station in 1965 and was severely beaten, spending the next four years in Whitchurch Hospital before passing away in 1969.

Back on the A470, just north of the Abercynon roundabout, look up to the left and you'll see the Giant's Bite, a large gap in the ridge. To those in touch with mythology's weave, it was a hurried bite taken in passing by a peckish giant. To those with their feet deep in cold, boring, earthy research, it is the remains of a quarry on the summit of Darren y Celyn, Holy Ridge, that supplied stone for the Edwardsville Viaducts nearby.

Continuing past the infamous Aberfan slurry slide, a left sweep brings into view the vista and spread of Merthyr

Tydfil Town itself.

It used to be in the old County of Glamorgan, but is now a County Borough in its own right. Some say the re-organisation of the Welsh counties is a political plot to keep us confused and uncertain. First we had thirteen counties, then we had eight and now we have twenty-two, with new thoughts of reducing them down to six or so. When I suggested in a broadcast that I'm no longer entirely certain which county people live in, I had a response from a Bargoed man who resided in border country himself, as far as counties go: 'You are right, Roy, I've lived in four counties and I haven't moved house at all.'

In its heyday, Merthyr was the largest town in Wales, by far. The Industrial Revolution was given an impetus in fire here at the iron works of Dowlais, Cyfarthfa, Penydarren and Plymouth. George Borrow, in his book *Wild Wales*, published in 1862, described his introduction to the town thus: 'Turning round a corner at the top of a hill I saw blazes here and there and what happened to be a glowing mountain in the south east…so great was the light cast by the blazes and that wonderful glowing object, that I could distinctly see the little stones upon the road.'

Merthyr is a compendium of Welsh history, encompassing the early tribes, the Romans and their fort beneath Penydarren Football ground where the Martyrs play, the rural valley and then the industrial blast that was known worldwide. Admiral Nelson came here to see where his naval cannons were made, the world's first railway steam engine, developed by the Cornishman Richard Trevithick, trundled out of here, on its historic journey from Penydarren to Abercynon.

Immigrants came from several corners, Ireland, England, Spain and Italy. The town had an established Chinatown, but not a Chinatown as we would perceive it these days. There was no one Chinese in it and the area was more accurately called China, a name probably taken from the tales of the British opium wars with the country. It was a no-go area, a kind of forbidden city, a den of thieves, rogues and prostitutes, but it did have an emperor, one Shoni Sgugorfawr, 100 per cent Welsh apparently. It was suggested that police ventured into the area only when they were depressed and saw no future in life.

The Merthyr Rising in 1831 was a statement of intent from workers who suffered severe injustice. Alexander Cordell's novel *The Fire People* well suits the period. Magistrates and ironmaster were under siege in the Castle Hotel and the protesters controlled the town. Soldiers, called in from Brecon, clashed with rioters and several were killed from both sides. Others were arrested, including Richard Lewis, popularly known as Dic Penderyn. He was accused of stabbing a soldier and was hanged in Cardiff, at a spot just outside where Cardiff Indoor Market is now, for it was the site of Cardiff Jail in those days. Dic became known as the first working class martyr. It was a grave injustice and, to this day, efforts are made to obtain a posthumous pardon for Dic. It's a bit late, but it will put the record straight.

Standing in the town is the historic Red House, the old town hall. On its balcony once stood Keir Hardie, a Scotsman, giving his acceptance speech after his election in 1900 as the first ever Labour MP in Britain, representing

Merthyr and Aberdare.

Merthyr Tydfil is indeed an enormous encyclopaedia. There is so much that has been written of the place, its people, and its position in the world.

The A470 rolls on however. North, past Crawshay's desirable detached residence with its lovely park, Cyfarthfa Castle, a snip at £30,000 in 1824, to the Brecon Beacons. Incidentally, *cyfarthfa* means 'a place for dogs', it being a hunting ground for use with dogs before industrialisation.

In the mid-1950s a howl of protest rose over the notorious plan to drown the hamlet of Capel Celyn, north-west of Bala, for the building of Llyn Celyn Dam in the Treweryn River Valley. Sixty-seven Welsh speaking residents were to be displaced for the purpose of supplying Liverpool with water. Despite vigorous protests, Capel Celyn was destroyed and this action was to ignite a political change in the Welsh psyche. 'Cofiwch Treweryn' ('Remember Treweryn') has been a clarion call all the way to the establishment of the Welsh Assembly.

Less known is the fact that the self same action occurred in 1914, for the benefit of Cardiff's water supply. It was in the Taff Valley, just north of Merthyr Tydfil, alongside the A470. Three reservoirs were built, the nearest to Merthyr being Llwyn Onn Reservoir. Under the waters of Llwyn Onn lie two hamlets, Ynysyfelin and Nantddu. The community of Ynysyfelin consisted of farms, small holdings, the Red Lion Arms, Pwllcoch woollen mill, a school and a chapel. Bethel Chapel still survives, having been built at Llwyn Onn, two miles from Cefn Coed on the outskirts of Merthyr Tydfil.

Nantddu lost St Mary's Church, the vicarage and a number of pubs, including the Tredegar Arms. A large swathe of land was owned by Lord Tredegar, who had a hunting lodge in the area which survives today as the Nant Ddu Hotel. You can contemplate these drowned communities and the displaced people as you dine in the hotel or, if you pull in to the lay-by alongside Llwyn Onn reservoir, you can view the lake over a snack from the burger van which is usually in situ.

Pass the three reservoirs and you come to The Storey Arms. The original building was owned by Anthony Storey, a local land owner who had close connections with Clive of India, and one of his daughters married into the Dilwyn Pottery dynasty of Swansea. A lively livestock market was held there in the nineteenth century, but in the 1920s the inn was demolished. The name on the present building suggests it's a pub, but it isn't. It's the Brecon Beacons Activity Centre. The Storey Arms Centre is below the peaks of Corn Ddu and Pen y Fan, the two highest peaks in the south of Britain. They were formerly referred to as Cadair Arthur, Arthur's Seat. The topography tells you why.

Near the route to the centre is the poignant obelisk to Tommy Jones, just five years of age, whose body was found there in August 1900 after a twenty-nine day search. The son of a Rhondda miner, he was staying with his grandparents in the area when he apparently wandered off and died, probably of hyperthermia.

Passing The Storey Arms is the drovers' road from Merthyr Tydfil and it can be clearly seen from the A470 as it clings to the opposite side of the descending valley, heading for Libanus and the town of Brecon.

Brecon opens up a book of tales, true, mystical and mythical, from its hinterland to the wild expanse of the Beacons. Some are well-known, others add to the magic of the place and its ancient fables: The Lady of the Lake, The wild boar chase of Twrch Trwyth, black cats and fairies, the men in the cave, the Christmas Day massacre. These have been wonderfully weaved into a book by Horatio Clare, where his personal gloss gives a wondrous sheen to each patch of the mural.

As for us, well, we continue seeking lay-bys and stopping places along the road where stories, fact, fiction and fanciful, make the journey and the stopping worthwhile.

16. Discord Galore to Dinas Mawddwy

The A470/ Gwynedd

Headlong north from Brecon, with its nearby Roman fort, its castle and its fine Royal Welsh Regiment Museum, Zulu artefacts included, and the historic Christ College, on to the bonny banks of the River Wye beyond Llyswen. The Wye accompanies the road for miles and is an attractive, if distracting, presence.

The River Wye flows from the biggest watershed in Wales, so they say, the hefty, hulking lump of moorland traditionally known as one of The Three Welsh Mountains: Pumlumon. Plynlimon if you prefer the English version, either way it means five peaks. In the Cambrian Mountains, the range releases three major rivers, the Wye, the Severn, or Hafren, the longest river in Britain, and the Rheidol, which is quite short but makes its point.

The rivers cannot just quietly set off on their journey from their source. Oh no, there is a tale to their meanderings, the origin, as ever, lost in time, back to the Iron Age or beyond to the worship of water nymphs and goddesses. If Dad was Pumlumon, then his offspring, the three water nymphs, had adventure, spirit and a 'get up and go' restlessness within their every ripple.

Allegedly, they met one day on their father's hefty haunches to discuss how best to answer the call to the sea. The first sister, some say the youngest, decided, in impatience, to head west and take the shortest route. Quickly getting to the sea, she became known as Ystwyth (Rheidol). The second sister, the most beautiful of the three, enjoyed the landscape and journeyed sedately through attractive areas to arrive at the sea, under the name Wye. The third sister, the eldest, had no desire to rush like

Ystwyth, but she did have Wye's taste for exploration and for seeking out visits to the fairest cities of the land to see the wonders of mankind. Wandering was her way in life. This was the Severn.

I have to say that other folklore suggestions are available, if you wish to seek them out. One involves an early morning race where the Wye got away on time and meandered beautifully, always having her watery goal in mind, the Severn got up later, got lost and really took the long route, and Rheidol overslept and was left rushing to the coast as fast as the flow would take her.

On the A470, alongside the Wye from Llyswen to Builth Wells, you do have a choice. If seeking refreshment, try the refurbished Erwood Railway Station. It is a tea house, a gallery and three Great Western Railway carriages are parked at the platform, but, in crossing the Wye, take care at one bridge. It is so narrow that, even in a car, you have to breathe in sharply to avoid touching the sides.

Builth Wells is famous for the Royal Welsh Agricultural Show but has other attractions, and if you are seeking out the castle it is opposite the Wye Theatre but behind the roadside buildings. The old motte-and-bailey Norman design is now exactly that...a mound and ditch. Most if not all of the stonework has been purloined over the years for a little bit of garden wall here, a small dwelling there, and, in one or two cases, it is suggested, for an extension to a farm, cowshed or even a mini-manor of a gentleman's residence. This was not, of course, over the period of the Dark Ages, but, in truth, it was dark enough for the purpose.

If interest overcomes you, don't go directly over the

River Wye bridge; take a detour to a lay-by out on the Llandovery Road. The lay-by lies in Cilmeri and just beyond the pub, The Prince Llewelyn, there is a memorial stone. The pub's name gives a fair clue as to who the memorial commemorates. Llewelyn ap Gruffudd was the last true Prince of Wales, before that title was re-used by 'Longshanks', Edward I.

In those days, there was a distinct lack of brotherly love about and an overkill, literally, of mishap. Lots of bad blood and bad luck. To put it nicely, but precisely, Llewelyn's father, Gruffudd, was Llewelyn the Great's eldest son, but he had been born on the other side of the blanket (illegitimate), so when the elder Llewelyn died the title passed to his younger brother, Dafydd ap Llewelyn. Dafydd kept Gruffudd prisoner, then, under pressure, gave his custody over to Henry III of England. Gruffudd was held in the Tower of London but attempted to escape from a high window, slipped, and fell to his death. Dafydd then rebelled against Henry III and Llewelyn, for reasons known only to himself, joined the rebellion.

When Dafydd died without an heir, Llewelyn grabbed his chance. Things went pretty well until Llewelyn's younger brother, another Dafydd, came of age and stretched his horizons. He befriended Henry III, was intoxicated by ambition and, to cut a long story short and the list of skirmishes shorter, Llewelyn was branded a rebel. To put another ingredient into the *cawl*, Henry III died and 'Longshanks', Eddie I, came on stage, encouraging Dafydd to have a go at his brother. In time, however, Dafydd decided to be a rebel himself and set himself up to face the English. Llewelyn, unwisely, decided to support the upstart.

In December 1282, events took a turn for the worse. At the Battle of Orewin Bridge at Cilmeri, the English got the upper hand and Llewelyn, who was not present at the kick-off, hurried to Builth Wells Castle to rally support. He was unsuccessful and, on his return to Cilmeri, pure bad luck jumped on his saddle. He appears to have run into enemy knights who attacked and killed him. He had not been wearing any obvious coat of arms, so the knights didn't know the significance of their successful private set-to. Later in the day he was identified and his head taken to London as proof of the success and set up above the gate of Tower of London on the point of a lance.

So, the detour and the monument near The Prince Llewelyn pub lead to a small lay-by but a big story.

On from Builth Wells you enter Rhayader, where, further west, in quiet country, lie the impressive Elan Valley Dams. It's worth a sidestep for a view. Of course, these dams are associated with early training by 617 Squadron of the RAF prior to Operation Chastise, the attack on the Ruhr Dams of Germany led by Wing Commander Guy Gibson. Early tests on the depth required for the explosions, later developed into the famed 'bouncing bomb', were carried out on the temporary Nant y Gro masonry dam.

As an added link to the Dambusters, it's worth visiting Penarth Pier, which has been wonderfully renovated. At the top floor there is a room dedicated to the 617 Squadron. Guy Gibson married Evelyn Mary Moore, a Penarth showgirl dancer, in 1940 at All Saints Church and made 21 Archer Road, Penarth their home. There is a plaque dedicated to Gibson in the room, as there is for young Gordon Yeo from Barry, a front gunner in another Lancaster bomber on the raid that was sadly shot down, killing all crew members.

Resolutely onwards, ever onwards, on the northbound A470 to Llangurig, and a question... Is Llangurig really the geographical centre of Wales? It has been claimed as such. If not, then where is the centre spot?

The A470 has many quirks, one of which is the drastic turn it takes from a seemingly obvious track. It does it between Brecon and Builth Wells, when a left turn takes you off at right angles when the natural route would seemingly be to Hay-on-Wye. It does it again as you near Newtown, just to keep you on your toes, shooting off suddenly at Caersws and heading north-west for Carno, once famed for the production of Laura Ashley domestic and personal artistry and apparel, then Llanbrynmair, where the moorland back road from Llanidloes, through Staylittle, joins the main artery. That rural road is very picturesque, undulating past Llyn Clywedog, the Clywedog reservoir. There are extraordinary views to wonder at there, but it is as well to remember that protests against the construction were vociferous, including a bomb explosion in the construction site in 1966.

As for Staylittle and the reason for the name set in this summer grazing land where there are several houses named, in part, Hafod (summer dwelling), there was an inn on the old drovers' road called 'Stay a little'. Next door to the inn was a smithy, and the blacksmith brothers who worked there were so adept and fast at shoeing horses that a longer stay than 'a little' was unnecessary.

These place names have their stories in-built. An example from the south-west, in Pembrokeshire, is Stepaside, so named after Oliver Cromwell passed through on his way to Pembroke and Ireland and locals were asked to make way, or 'Stepaside', as his army marched. On the other hand, there are three narrow bridges locally and people who confront others on the road have to 'stepaside'. So, take your pick...but I prefer the former explanation.

On from Llanbrynmair and you head for Cemmaes Road, later passing Aberangell as you near Dinas Mawddwy. Look out, by the way, for the dragon, the cafe with incredible wooden working models and the rabbit small holding. As you approach the village, there is a roundabout where the A458 from Welshpool and Shrewsbury will join you, and you see the Brigands Inn on your right. Park at the inn and face west with the front door behind you and you will be facing Camlann, the site of King Arthur's last battle. Imagine the Britons on the upper slope of the hill and the Saxons coming along the old Welshpool track and you have the scene set. The Brigands Inn is on the front line.

Background information on the main players and events of the sixth-century battle is sketchy and confused, but it adds to the drama. Had Arthur been in France chasing Lancelot, who was having an affair with his loved one, Guinevere? Why is it reported in some annals that Mordred, notorious traitor that he was, had designs on Arthur's kingdom and had also started an affair with Guinevere? Where did she have the time for these dalliances? The battle resulted in the deaths of both Mordred and Arthur, and, to add further confusion, some say they were fighting on the same side. Ty Derw House is on the battlefield, so was breakfast at this B&B a lively, disrupted affair when the battle kicked off?

Mordred was killed outright, but Arthur, though mortally injured, lasted a while. He instructed Sir Bedivere (Bedwyr) to throw his sword, Excalibur, into the nearby lake. Bedivere reported to Arthur that he'd done it, but nothing unusual had occurred. Arthur was having none of it and insisted he do it again. This time the Lady of the Lake stretched up her hand to grasp the sword and slowly took it down beneath the water. Following Arthur's passing, he was layed on a barge which was guided across the water by maidens to the Isle of Avalon.

Was there such a lake? Well, Dinas Mawddwy, or Minllyn as it's known too, meaning edge of the lake, gives a clue that there was once an expanse of water.

Questions remain. Was this the correct Camlann? There are other candidates nearby, and in other parts of Wales, as well as in Somerset, Cornwall and Scotland. It was once strongly suggested to me by a passionate Welshman that, as a nation, we should quickly decide where the lake was and then construct a bronze arm sticking out of the water, grasping Excalibur. It would be great for tourism and if we don't do it soon the Cornish might warm to the idea and see it through.

There is, however, a monument to Arthur that can be visited on the battlefield site. You have to enter the car park of the Meirion Woollen Mill to get to it, so take care, because although the mill is a very welcoming place, the car park is locked around 4.30 or 5 p.m.

Is it right? That remains the main question about the story and setting. History is usually written by the victor and archives were often penned hundreds of years after the event, so stories became subjective with romance and colour thrown in to add to the panorama in the mind. One has to always check things out, as far as possible. The quests continue, but intrigue and interest are still fired, so you don't ever want too much cold water thrown on a tale...it dampens or extinguishes the excitement. Truth and pragmatism are fine, but sometimes they don't half fill the boring bucket.

Yet, I am the patron of a new organisation in Aberdare, The Galapagos Club. We wear maroon jumpers with a golden turtle as a badge and a Latin logo: 'Hoc Non Credo'... 'I don't believe it'! At the moment it is made up of far in the past rugby club members of Aberdare RFC and functions to support the club and teams. However, it has potential. 'Hoc Non Credo' and the Galapagos Club could spread and be a powerful lobbying force for good...forever questioning, persistently challenging authority at all levels. Members could be latter-day Knights of the Round Table, only there would be a busload of us, roaming the countryside, doing good and righting wrongs. At our age, though, saving damsels in distress would be a delegated responsibility.

To return to Arthur's Camlann, but to move on in history, the Dinas Mawddwy area is also famous as a place of vagabonds and brigands. The law of the land was something that many locals did not subscribe to and the Red Bandits of Mawddwy became infamous. In one incident, the Sheriff of Meirionnydd, Baron Lewis ap Owen, was murdered. Several were hanged for the crime and it was rumoured that John Coch (John Goch ap Gruffudd ap Huw, or Red John), was the one who struck the fatal blow. Quite a few 'aps' in his name, so thanks must be given for small mercies, for it would have been hell filling in the daily school register in later years.

The story goes that the Baron had arrested many bandits in a previous venture and that two brothers had gone to the gallows, one being particularly young. Their mother pleaded for their lives, but the Baron would have none of it. She flew into a rage and supposedly ripped open her clothing and screamed, 'These breasts have given suck to those who shall wash their hands in your blood.' It turned out to be a pretty effective curse.

Many places have names that rekindle memories of those days of banditry, like Llety'r Lladron (robbers' lodging) or Llety Gwylliaid (bandits' lodging). Inns were associated as gathering places for these characters. The Brigands Inn, earlier known as Bury's Hotel, was a candidate, as was the famed and much older Red Lion of Dinas Mawddwy itself, near the site of the lake where Excalibur was allegedly thrown.

Climbing away from what is a very attractive area, the A470 rises steeply over a ridge that in my mind is one definitive gateway to north Wales. The landscape changes suddenly. On reaching the top, the mountains of Snowdonia in the distance give a clear vision of the rugged and enthralling journey to come. It's no wonder that the

A470 was dubbed Britain's most attractive road in 2014, weaving through the Brecon Beacons in the south and the Snowdon range in the north.

Jeremy Clarkson and his team on *Top Gear* also included the western reaches of the Brecon Beacons as meriting a gold star, dubbing the A4069 from Brynaman to Llangadog over the Black Mountain one of the most testing yet attractive roads they had driven on. Added to the twists and turns are cuckoo bend, the flashing-by scenery, and the kamikaze sheep who wait at the side of the road until you are upon them before deciding that the grass is greener on the other side. These sheep are a branch of the Valleys or Nelson sheep that Dai Jones of Llanilar, famed presenter of S4C farming programmes, describes as having innate, almost Neolithic age minds of their own. They are only ever controllable, so he suggests, in a freezer...with the lid closed.

Back to the A470 ridge north of Dinas Mawddwy and Snowdon and its hinterland form the backdrop as the road drops towards Dolgellau. To the west of the town, and clearly seen, is the legendary mountain Cadair Idris, Idris' Chair. There await more stories, more mythological meanderings, more facts, and more fanciful, elasticated tales...especially if you decide to spend the night upon it.

17. The Chair —
Myths in Mind,
Poetry in Soul

Gwynedd

'There's gold in them thar hills'...an excited cry from America's panning for gold days, but in this case it's Dolgellau, or nearby, anyway.

Dolgellau is a small market town lying alongside the River Wnion and the A470 trailway. The Wnion, incidentally, is a tributary of the River Mawddach, which enters the sea with aplomb in a stunning estuary and Barmouth's fine briny and beachy welcome.

Dolgellau has an interesting town square and stands solidly built of the local dark grey dolerite stone. To the west is the brooding bulk of Cadair Idris, one of Wales's iconic mountains. There was a time you could have been ridden up a distance on a mule, but you'd be hard pushed to find one these days. Still, alternative access to the heights are available and legendary tales await. Cadair Idris, for now, will also await, as we hist and hark that cry for gold.

Well, there was a minor gold rush in the nineteenth century and the local gold mines, at one time, employed 500 men. Clogau St David's mine in Bontddu and Gwynfynydd mine in Ganllwyd, in the Dolgellau gold belt, have supplied gold for many Royal weddings.

Prior to the Roman invasion, this was the land of the Ordovices, a Celtic tribe who held the freehold in mid- and north-west Wales. They were one of the few tribes in Britain that resisted the Romans with a will, destroying a Roman cavalry squadron in one serious skirmish. Bad move, big repercussions. The Roman governor took umbrage to an extreme and, according to Tacitus, the script-writer, the Ordovices could have been wiped out but for the helpful terrain and upland hideaways. The Ordovices were led by Caradog, who had a kind of 'leadership certificate, will travel' nuisance arrangement to giving the Romans bad days, because he had also been in the south whipping up support from the ever-ready Silures tribe.

Flicking through the annual calendars, a visit to Dolgellau by George Fox, who founded the religious Society of Friends, the Quakers, in 1657, resulted in many of the inhabitants converting to Quakerism. The gradual and growing reaction and persecution of this group led to a large number emigrating to Pennsylvania in 1686, under the leadership of Robert Ellis. The Pennsylvania town of Bryn Mawr, home to the prestigious women's liberal arts college, is named after Ellis' farm, near Dolgellau. This is the true origin of that name, for there have been suggestions that there might have been a link with Brynmawr, the Heads of the Valleys town and the expanding iron and coal industries a century or so later.

Oddly, my main link with Dolgellau also has a religious back-drop. It was a television filming undertaking at the Carlmelite Convent, the Monastery of the Holy Spirit and our Lady of Peace. The sisters there follow Saint Albert of Jerusalem. It is a closed order, so closed at the time that one wondered who took the bins out for the weekly refuse collection.

The convent is on a hill, leading out of the town. They were warm in their welcome and the ambience was peace personified. We, however, had a catalyst for complication in our midst: our television director. He was a Celt, an easily excitable Celt from Northern Ireland, who, when vexed or frustrated, had a problem with word evacuation;

the substitute words his brain seized upon had a colour and Anglo Saxon origin from centuries before the Saxons hit the shores of southern England. One tirade, let loose behind a wall in a quiet part of the Convent garden because of a faulty camera, saw our jaws drop...and our eyes close, too, when we realised that four of the Sisters were sitting in contemplation, if not prayer, behind the wall.

His demeanour definitely subsided and cooled in the following weeks, so the rest of the film crew concluded that the Sisters behind the wall must have put in a series of very effective group prayers pleading for his verbal temperance; fair play to them.

Cadair Idris, the Chair of Idris, lies, often in a moody, melancholy light, to the west of the town. It has three peaks: Pen y Gadair, the Head of the Chair, Cyfrwy, the Saddle, and Mynydd Moel, the Bare Mountain. Half way down the mountain, a cwm is filled by a stunning and apparently bottomless glacial lake, Llyn Cau, home of a Welsh dragon who terrorised the locals but was captured by King Arthur (yes, he got about quite a bit), who dragged him to the lake and released him there. In fact, there are apparently quite a few bottomless lakes in the Cadair Idris area, Llyn Mwyngul, more commonly known as Tal-y-Llyn Lake, being a very noted one. Cadair Idris is sometimes called Arthur's Seat, but Edinburgh has one of those too, so we'll allow them to bask in their own story, for we know the real truth.

Who was Idris, then? A giant, an astronomer, a poet and a prince, apparently. It is said that, on feeling some annoying grit in his shoe, he removed the shoe and threw the grit all over the place. One piece fell as a hefty rock in Aberllefenni, another at Rhydymain, yet another in Abergeirw and two other large stones near the road as you head for Dolgellau. As a bonus, two other stones feature, one thrown across the road near a lay-by and another, slightly smaller one, put there by his wife, probably a brawny weightlifter of a girl in her own right, judging by its size.

Two words of warning. There is the legend that Cadair Idris forms part of the hunting ground of Gwyn ap Nudd, lord of the Celtic underworld known as Annwen. If you ever hear them howling, it really isn't great news for long-term insurance premiums, so try and put the howls down to atmospheric interference. Finally, if you are hell-bent on spending the night on the mountain, it is foretold that come the morn you will either come down a poet or completely off your head.

As for the lore of mountains, I have come across the odd eyebrow raiser. I was once regaled by Dai the Gate, a local character in Upper Brynaman, so named because his family had once lived in a past toll gate. He was a full-time but lapsed collier, grave-digger and a 'thrower -in' of concessionary coal for widows who had a ton delivered to their door, loose, no bags. He was also a part-time philosopher and a student of the human condition who lived in our terraced street, and he told me, solemnly, that if a man was ever found walking the hills on his own, it quickly got around the village that he was depressed.

I seem to always attract such characters. I must have the face of a priest or a man of the cloth, for people sometimes seem to seek me out for 'confession'. They tell me things they must regret the following day. I look in the mirror and I ask, 'Is that face really wholesome and trustworthy?' There are the oddities as well. On the subject of mountains and roaming or hiking, I was once told by a serious fell walker that if I was lost I should seek out a cow. He reckoned that if a cow has nothing more pressing to do, they will stand and face north, always north. Ridiculous, I know, if only for the fact the you rarely find cows roaming freely on high fells; sheep quite often, but cows, no.

Onwards from Dolgellau, the A470 rises to a plateau where the road rushes past Trawsfynydd towards the dramatic, well-worked and craggy slate slopes of Blaenau Ffestiniog. To the the west are seen the high, steep hills, aspiring to be mountains, of Rhinog Fawr, Diffwys and Y Llethr, and it's well worth calling in at Trawsfynydd.

Beyond the village is a large, man-made lake, Llyn Trawsfynydd, which was built in the early 1920s to supply water for a local hydro-electric power station. It involved the drowning of some two dozen properties, some of historical significance, but there seemed little objection at the time, the new power station being regarded, generally, as a good thing. As you pass the village going north, another architectural edifice comes into view, a place that needed cooling water from the lake for twin reactors in its time. It would be fair to say that it is, perhaps, not an architectural prize winner, for it stands there, solid, austere, with a hint of the television series *Quatermass* about it. It is the Trawsfynydd Nuclear Power Station, now de-commissioned, but there are official thoughts of possible resurrection... Who knows?

In the village there is a memorial statue to Ellis Humphrey Evans, 'Hedd Wyn', a shepherd and Welsh language poet who was killed on the first day of the Battle of Passchendaele, in Flanders, six weeks before his poem won the Bardd Chair, the Bard's Chair, at that year's National Eisteddfod. The Chair was sent to his parents, draped in the black cloth placed upon it after the announcement was made in the eisteddfod at Birkenhead. It is now on display at his family's home farm, Yr Ysgwrn, or 'The Bone'.

Hedd Wyn was a Christian pacifist and did not initially enlist. The First World War left Welsh non-conformists deeply divided. But the war inspired him to write his most noted poetry, including *Plant Trawsfynydd* (*Children of Trawsfynydd*), *Y Blotyn Du* (*The Black Dot*), and *Rhyfel* (*War*), which is often quoted.

Hedd Wyn did eventually enlist to prevent his brother being called up to the services. When he was allowed home for necessary summer farm work the weather was inclement, he over-stayed his leave, was regarded a deserter and jailed before finally being returned to his regiment. He had written his National Eisteddfod entry, *Yr Arwr* (*The Hero*), in the summer, but in the rush to return to the front he forgot the poem and had to write it again, so now two copies survive. He joined the 15th Battalion Royal Welsh Fusiliers, part of the 38th Welsh Division, and was killed at Pilkem Ridge on the first day of the Battle of Passchendaele. Among the other fatalities that day was the Irish war poet Francis Ledwidge. Both are buried in Artillery Wood Cemetery, near Langemark, just a few miles from Ypres.

It was my privilege to be the host at the commemorative 100th Anniversary Service of Remembrance on 31st July 2017 at Pilkem Ridge, Langemark, Belgium. The vast areas of Flanders, encompassing so many cemeteries, release two emotions: sadness to the depths and anger to the surface; anger at the sheer waste and human cost, on both sides.

Back over the centuries and The Mabinogi, the mythological tales told from oral tradition in the eleventh century, turns a page near Trawsfynydd. Our heroine, Blodeuwedd, surfaces in the fourth branch of the Mabinogi.

A man named Lleu has been cursed. He will never marry a human wife. Two magicians concoct a plan to get around this vexing problem and make a wife for Lleu out of flowers. Her name is Blodeuwedd, which means, literally, 'flower face'. They settle down in a castle near Trawsfynydd, until Blodeuwedd, hit by temptation and a wandering eye, has an ill-advised extra-curricular fling with the Lord of Penllyn, modern day Bala. In revenge, she's hunted down to Llyn Morwynion, the 'Lake of the Maidens', near Blaenau Ffestiniog and turned into an owl.

Factual history includes the Romans at their fort, the remote Tomen y Mur, near Trawsfynydd. Recycling has been done over the years, as was the habit, and some of the stones from the fort found their way to Harlech Castle. One, commemorating the completion of a section of wall by 'Marcus and the boys' is in-built to a pub in Maentwrog. On to slate country.

18. To the Viking Alligator, the UN and Port Wrexham

Llandudno
Conwy

Think Welsh slate and communities in Wales leap to mind: Penrhyn, near Bethesda, Dinorwic, near Llanberis, at one time the two largest slate quarries in the world, as well as the Nantlle Valley Quarries and Blaenau Ffestiniog, the largest slate mine in the world. Each one has its story, Penrhyn adding a bitter three-year strike to its saga.

On the road's journey north, just after leaving Trawsfynydd, the A470 indulges in one of its quirks. You head straight on down the hill, seemimgly towards Porthmadoc and possibly Portmeirion, when, all of a sudden, there is a sharp turn and the A470 heads for Blaenau Ffestiniog, deep slate country.

In its day the largest town in Meirioneth, Blaenau Ffestiniog carved its powerful place in Welsh industrial history and even today the remnants of the mine's past workings dramatically scar the steep, rugged hills around the town. Everywhere you look, life's colour is dabbed with a double dollop of grey. The slate, in huge slabs, comes down almost to the very door of the cottages. The remains and spoil heaps are everywhere. There is drama in the sight you see and a foreboding, a danger, because it was a hard industry in every possible way. You cannot fail to be moved by the abandoned sites and thoughts of what went on here: the men, their life, their religion, and their need, through the strenuous physical tasks, for enlightenment, for culture, even to the point of holding mini-eisteddfodau underground by the light of their candles, in most instances bought out of their pay.

Take a journey on one of the Great Little Trains of Wales, the Ffestiniog Railway, the 'Ivor the Engine Line' of television animation fame. On the route that the slate was taken to Porthmadog many years ago, make a request stop at Coed y Bleiddiau, 'The Wood of Wolves'. Local legend has it that the last wolf in Wales met its end here. There is a cottage nearby, the residents obtaining their provisions by holding out a basket, complete with list and money, to the guard of the 'up' train and receiving the full basket from the 'down' train without stopping, though it may slow down a bit.

One tenant at the cottage was Harry St. John Bridger Philby, the father of Kim Philby, the infamous KGB agent and traitorous spy. Philby Jr is thought to have visited the cottage often and his father had been a friend of William Joyce, Lord Haw-Haw, the notorious broadcaster of *Germany Calling* during the Second World War. Joyce is said to have visited the cottage twice and referred to it in his broadcasts; though neither his visits or those of Kim Philby can be ratified, they surely took place...if only for the sake of the story!

Blaenau Ffestiniog these days has tourist attractions, if you fancy the exciting Zip Wire Journey or the Bounce Below giant underground trampolines and, of course, the visits to Llechwen Slate Caverns. Llechwen is still a working quarry, but in a small way; like the slate industry, the population has severely declined. I have to say though, that each time I travel through the town I feel a respect and reverence for those who made their mark in this place and took Wales, in slate, to the world.

Rising away from the town, the mountain ridge points you down to another world, towards Betws-y-Coed and passing Dolwyddelan and its castle, one which I fell off once. It's more of a dominating tower than a castle and my fall was not far...thank heavens. Serious mountain climbing is not on my CV, and neither are walls of any height above my own.

Betws-y-Coed, 'Prayer house in the wood', has been described as one of the honeypot locations in Snowdonia. It has many hotels and craft shops, mostly built in the nineteenth century, its own Waterloo Bridge built by Thomas Telford and embossed 1815, the year Napoleon was defeated at Trafalgar, and it was on the Irish Mail route from London to Holyhead. The River Conway has attractive waterfalls there, including the much visited Swallow Falls, just up the A5 towards Capel Curig and Bangor.

In terms of tales and legends, try the Anna Davies country wear store or the Royal Oak Hotel. Both are said to be haunted. In the store, a cloaked lady has, on occasion, made herself a nuisance by throwing boots at staff, but we are going back to the 1950s and 1960s, so she may have found a pair to fit her by now. In the hotel, there were reports of whispering in the corridors, televisions switching themselves on and off and doors slamming by themselves. There may be simple explanations, but I hold an open mind, especially after my experience at a birthday party in an ancient coaching inn in Kent. In a crowded lounge, I was not alone in noticing a half-full pint glass lift from the mantlepiece, pour its beer contents down the back of a guest and then return to its podium. A presence? Possibly, or was it that my ale was very good too? I won't even mention being woken up in the night to the sound of flapping wings in the chimney of the bedroom fireplace.

Heading towards the coast you pass through Llanrwst, a small town with an interesting, narrow centre. 'Tidy', as we say in Wales. It has almshouses, the church of St Grwst, which holds the stone coffin of Llewelyn the Great and Pont Fawr, and a narrow three arch stone bridge, designed by Inigo Jones, so it is said, in 1636.

The intriguing thing is that, allegedly, Llanrwst Council sought a seat on the United Nations Security Council, as an independent state within Wales in 1947. It wasn't successful, and no proof can be found in the UN Security Council minutes. That's a pity... Someone should read them again to make sure.

Down the road and 'round several bends, which is often the case in Wales, for Welsh miles are longer than the measured mathematical norm, you pass the well-nurtured and natured Bodnant Gardens and, eventually, Conway Castle comes into view across the river. It's an impressive fortification, one of Edward I's ring of iron around Wales, or, more correctly, ring of stone. Conway is Conwy in Welsh and the place name is dotted worldwide. There are at least eighteen Conways globally, not counting a lake, a river, a national park, the Rolls Royce Conway, the first turbo-fan aircraft engine and a Conway variant of the Centurion tank. Popular name.

Thomas Telford built a railway bridge next to the castle, modelling the turrets on the many designed by Edward I's architects. For those into spirits, there was a monastery near the castle and apparently, now and again, two hooded, robed monks have been seen loitering and hovering about. On the more earthly plane, people born inside the town walls of Conway are known as jackdaws. The town also has the smallest house in Britain down near the quay at just six feet wide, and it is claimed that the marshy spit on the land on the west side of the estuary was the location where golf was first played on Welsh soil. There may be other claimants to that, of course.

At last, at last, to journeys end and a well earned rest for the A470. Within a few miles of Conway is the place that came within an ace of being named Port Wrexham: Llandudno. Why Port Wrexham? Well, in the 1850s, the St. George Harbour and Railway Company planned to develop the area as an export base for Denbighshire coal. Port Wrexham was regarded as a suitable name for the expanding town, but in the latter half of the nineteenth century tourism possibilities really began to make headway and the name Llandudno stuck.

Tudno, who was to give his name to the town, was a monk who established an oratory on the Great Orme. Legends say that the name 'Orme' derives from 'heva horma', a reference by the Vikings to the promontory's serpent-like shape. Although the Vikings knew this area well, they did not pillage the early community because they were frightened by the protective 'alligator'. If you look at the Great Orme from the east, especially at dusk, the landmass does resemble a large and powerful predator which looks out to sea. On the eastern side of the bay, the Little Orme is stated to be the 'elephant'. As the tide goes out, you can see the elephant's trunk lift from the water, a possible double whammy for the wisely wary Vikings.

The area did have quite a notoriety in later history, especially the Little Orme, as a very busy and productive place for smuggling. The Great Orme, of course, became the epicentre of the copper trade in Europe during the Bronze Age. There were six kilometres of tunnels, many nearly 4000 years old, some of them so small that only children could have dug them.

This always throws a conundrum up in my mind with regard to the trading of the early ages. It is a naïve question, but I'll ask it anyway. How did one people know of the other, sometimes far off, people? And how did they know of their products, their usefulness and whether they were amenable? How did the early news travel? Did someone, in other areas of Britain, or indeed Europe, ever really come up with the suggestion, 'Hey, I'll tell you what's good for what you need...copper. I know where you can get copper. It will change your life, I'm telling you.' Early trading and contact and how both developed has always fascinated me.

One of the most famous caves on the Great Orme is the man-made Llech or Hiding Cave, which was built 400 years ago in a natural fissure. The cave is hexagonal, a stone bench runs along the interior wall and in the centre is a stone pedestal that once held a table. The cave's purpose is a mystery, apart from a clue in *Cywydd i'r Llech yn Llandudno*, a poem from the seventeenth century. There is a suggestion that part of the structure is now buried. The poet Siôn Dafydd Las also said, 'it was repaired with skill and taste for Mostyn's Heir, a man of wit', a reference to

Mostyn's family, who controlled much of north Wales and later developed the Mostyn Estate.

You can ride a tram or a cable car up the Great Orme these days and look down at a townscape that nearly had two piers. Prevarication put paid to the second one, out where the Venue Cymru Entertainment Centre is now; it never got built. That's the trouble with committees, I suppose. We Welsh are probably the world champions in committees. There is no greater moment in a Welsh committee than when it spawns a sub-committee and prevarication is pushed further along the table. There are guidelines, of course. One committee chairman of years' standing once gave me a piece of advice: 'Remember, committees are like life in general; never argue with an idiot, they will always bring you down to their level...and then beat you with experience.'

The Kashmiri goats of the Great Orme are esteemed indeed, the first two having been introduced to the area by Lord Mostyn. Queen Victoria was given a pair as a gift and they were made instantly fashionable by the aristocracy. The Royal Welsh Fusiliers have obtained most of their regimental goat mascots from the Great Orme, the regiment having historical connections to the town. Although all goats, having cloven hoofs, are associated with the devil, they also, apparently, bring great good luck, and also tend to be good prophets of the weather, moving uphill when fair weather is forecast and down when the clouds gang up from the west.

Looking down from the Great Orme, it is worth noting that the waters of Llandudno Bay, in their calmness on fair days, cover the remains of over thirty ships. The waters also hold a tale of an enemy visit in 1913, when two German submarines, the U-27 and U-38, lurked offshore in an attempt to rescue three German officers who had escaped from a prisoner of war camp at Dyffryn Aled, near Llansannan. The U-38 waited three nights in all, but the rescue attempt failed. After the war, the escaped officers learnt that they had been waiting in the wrong cove. They were quite cool in their attempt, it has to be said, for one of them, Hermann Tholens, even entered a barber, a tobacconist's shop for a packet of cigarettes and The Cocoa House, where he ordered coffee and cake. Their accents were quite thick and they were eventually caught, the other two, Wolff-Dietrich Baron von Helldorff and Heinig von Hennig, being apprehended when they were picked up by a taxi driver and driven straight to the headquarters of the Royal Welsh Fusiliers.

The story resonates with many who may remember the escape by German officers from the Island Farm prisoner of war camp, near Bridgend, during the Second World War. A few even got to Bridgend station. A U-boat commander and a Luftwaffe pilot tried to steal a doctor's car and when it wouldn't start they unbelievably, got four guards returning to Island Farm to help push it. One was apprehended and taken for safe keeping to the post office in Glais, near Clydach in the Swansea Valley. These are stories for another adventure.

On to a story and fanciful tale, earmarked for children, and back to Llandudno. It is well known that Alice and her Wonderland was inspired there, when Alice Liddell lived in the town in the 1860s and Charles Lutwidge Dodgson, using the pseudonym Lewis Carroll, visited her family at a residence which is now the St Tudno's Hotel. The rabbit hole that was used in the story is not historically marked, of course. The sequel film, *Alice Through the Looking Glass*, came later.

As for glass, it's not so much a looking glass but a rear-view mirror and a windscreen that now come to mind, as we rewind the journey north with its tales and meanderings. *Down The Road and Round The Bend* has been a constant concentration on the A470 north-south main artery, each lay-by and pull-in loading the car boot with a compendium of tales of Wales, fact, fiction, fanciful and fulsome. Time then to re-fill the tank, gird ourselves up, draw a deep, fresh breath and move on, horizon bound, whether it be another coastline, where the views are far, or to the high places, where the vistas are vast.

19. The Coffin Route

Llanddeusant to the Upper Swansea Valley

A Welsh *cwtch* is a cuddle, but one hundred per cent more. A *cwtch* is a warm, comforting, safe place. Of course, a cwtch can mean a different thing according to circumstances.

There is the physical cwtch, the embrace from a loved one, or from someone to make you feel better and more secure, or, sometimes, from someone you haven't seen for a long time. As a baby, a *cwtch* was given an added warmth and security if it came supported by a Welsh shawl, wrapped around your mam and yourself in such a way that, although it bonded mother and child tightly, it still allowed your mother one arm free to do other things.

Then there was the safe, secure place like the 'cwtch' under the stairs, usually with a door to close on the cupboard. There was even the 'coal cwtch', where the supply of household coal was kept.

My *mamgu*, or grandmother, had certain set procedures if she felt the family was threatened. When there was a thunderstorm she would order us to gather in the 'cwtch' under the stairs. As children, we loved it. It was exciting. She would also make sure, during a particularly nasty storm, that the back door or front door of the house was left open. She would say, 'If a flash of lightning sends a bolt down our chimney, that open door makes sure that it's got a way out...otherwise there will be mayhem here.'

That habit of hers took years to seep out of my system. For a couple of decades I felt that her advice and procedure made admirable sense. One habit I still adhere to even now, the business of closing the curtains as soon as it shows signs of getting dark of an evening. My wife, Elaine, finds it irritating because it shuts the day out abruptly.

I can understand that, but my mamgu's habit is deeply ingrained. As soon as the twilight started taking on a darker hue, the curtains in the living room would be drawn. Her reasoning seemed a bit drastic but we all had to bow to her experience and logic. She would declare, 'If your curtains are open when it gets to 'stop tap' in the Derlwyn Arms and someone sends a stone through your window, it will be your fault, because the men on their way home will just think you're being a busy-body, just watching to see who's drinking these days.' Strange logic, but it must have come from some past experience, possibly of another place in a different time.

So, to a cwtch that came as a surprise to me. It passed me by when it was given just a very few years ago. It was a *cwtch* given to a bog, an ancient peat bog on the Black Mountain of Carmarthenshire. The word cwtch was given to a hand-knitted wool blanket made by visual artist Ann Jordan, started in 2009 and sewn with heather seed to help repair the peat on which it was placed. It was finally put in position in 2015. Indeed, Ann was delighted that the blanket was returned to the earth from whence it came, from the local Black Mountain sheep.

The actual spot was located in the Bronze Age burial cairns of Carau Garreg y Las, on the Llyn y Fignen Felen peat bog on the mountain. Resembling freshly fallen snow, the 20 foot round blanket contained 12 miles of yarn and 140,000 stitches.

Ann's project focused on such things as 'Mountain Spirit', a tale that combines fact and fiction, including mythological tales passed on through storytelling, and a

'Shrouded Shawl', a performance celebrating the cycle of life, death and re-birth. It was laid in one of the ancient burial cairns on the Black Mountain to pay tribute to an old walking track known as the 'coffin route'.

The route earned its name during the era when men from the farms of the Llanddeusant area left their locality and walked over the Black Mountain to find work in the iron works, coal mines and quarries of the Upper Swansea Valley, Ystradgynlais in particular. In the rural areas of Carmarthenshire it was the period of the Rebecca Riots and the notorious toll gates. Wool had reached rock-bottom prices and the Upper Swansea Valley was at the forefront of industrial development, being one of the major iron producing areas in Britain and Europe. It was in a later period that the Ynyscedwyn Works at Ystradgynlias was to be the base for David 'Papa' Thomas, who was instrumental in developing the hot blast method of iron production using the hard, local, anthracite coal. He later took his expertise to Pennsylvania to push forward iron production in America.

For the rural men of Llanddeusant and the wider rural areas, the Upper Swansea Valley was a magnet for work, for money and for uplifting them from the pressures of a hard country life of little reward. But, on occasion, this industrial work came at a tragic cost. Accidents were almost inevitable in these industries. Many lost their lives. News was taken back to their homelands and a sad traffic route was carved along the slopes of the Black Mountain. Those who had been killed were carried homeward by the men of Brynaman, and they were met halfway by the men of Llanddeusant, who carried the bodies onward so they could be laid to rest in the churchyards of St Simon and St Jude.

Centuries before, the Parliamentary Act of 1666 had decreed that all corpses should be buried in a woollen blanket in an attempt to save the British wool industry from foreign imports; the departed were subsequently always wrapped in woollen blankets. The final cwtch or return to their homes and families for the men carried over the mountain, has a strong resonance with the cwtch blanket used fairly recently to cover the peat bog on the same mountain when it was itself brought home to its final resting place, the place from whence it had originally come.

The coffin route has some similarity to the ancient corpse roads that were country wide in the United Kingdom. Sometimes they were called coffin roads, corpse ways, burial ways, lyks, or a lych way. They tended to be very difficult routes or paths, because the landowners did not want them to become standard passageways for trade or travel. Nor did they want the dead carried over fields, for fear, under the old superstitions, of guaranteeing a failed crop. Consequently, the routes were over rough moorland and so arduous that no one took them unless they really had to, in ferrying the dead. In many places, coffin stones were placed en-route as a resting spot for bearers. Some cemetery lychgates also have resting stones for the coffin as a quick breather spot before the final effort of carrying the deceased into the church.

These paths became steeped in folklore, with tales

of ghostly happenings along the way. Crossroads were particularly lively places for spirits because it was said that the world and underworld met at those points. The mourners and those ferrying the corpse tried to make it as difficult as possible for the spirits, in that they climbed over walls, over ditches, and particularly over water. Crossing streams, allegedly, really presented a spirit with a challenge, so it's as well to remember that in the face of some future coffin carrying expedition. You never know.

Corpse candles, balls of light or fire, were often seen, so it is said, travelling over the ground from the deceased's home to the cemetery. Of course, in the varying light of the day and early evening, barn owls can also appear luminous, but, in the emotional air of the journey, rationale is never carried along with the coffin.

Gerald of Wales, in the thirteenth century, related the story of a strange occurrence on a marble bridge leading from the church over the Alun rivulet at St Davids. The stone on the bridge was called Llech Llafar, the talking stone, because it once spoke as a corpse was carried over it to the cemetery. The effort of producing speech caused the stone to break, even though it was a hefty piece of rock, measuring ten feet long, five feet wide and one foot thick, although, to be fair, it had been worn quite smooth by the thousands who had walked over it. The bridge was replaced in the sixteenth century and the location of the original is not known these days.

Legend has it as well that Merlin, the magician, he of Arthurian legend, prophesied the death of an English king who had conquered Ireland on Llech Llafar. Prior to his death, he would be injured by someone with a red hand, according to Merlin, who had clearly decided to get down to the nitty gritty of fine detail in the telling of his tale. Henry II went on a pilgrimage to St Davids after travelling from Ireland and, on hearing the story, decided to test it out by crossing the bridge. No problem, not a scratch, no heart attack, not even a twinge. He denounced Merlin as a liar, but a bystander suggested that he, Henry II, might not be the king in the prophesy, and so it came to pass. Henry II never did conquer Ireland.

Myth, mysticism, folklore, the fanciful and also the indisputable fact all come together in a cawl, a broth, for this facet of Welsh life...death. Like most cultures in the world, we have our traditions, our theatre, our drama, our protocol.

Each family would have their memories, but funeral procedures covered common ground for most of us. When I was young, my grandmother had a neighbour. He had been diagnosed with a heart condition while still a young married man, so he could not work...officially. Dai Jones was a handy neighbour though, because, as hobbies, he was a home-based cobbler, as long as you brought your own leather, as well as a barber, with a scissors that hadn't really hit the edge of sharpness since the Romans flirted with the area but decided against it as non-priority in road planning. Still, however threatened Dai was by ill-health, he saw four coffins leave my grandmother's house before his time came.

All the funerals followed the same order of service, except perhaps my grandfather's day. He had been killed at Steer Pit, Gwaun Cae Gurwen, when I was seven, and there was an added depth to the poignancy of the occasion.

Immediately after a death, house curtains were drawn, with the neighbours drawing theirs in respect and sympathy. I found those days of almost permanent dusk in the house heavy to bear. The gap between death and burial was usually about three days. The minister or vicar would call in at the house to conduct a family service before the funeral. The non-conformist ministers were six-cylinder men, throwing *hwyl*, passion, despondency, a sense of loss, life's trials and tests, and the sudden wrench of parting into the cauldron of over-flowing emotion, like ingredients directly delivered from the Lord, with the minister as the ordained chef to bring all to the boil. If he hadn't got everyone quietly crying or loudly weeping on the first mix, he'd go around again.

Outside the door, the men stood. Only men, for women were not acceptable at a funeral in those days, even if the deceased was a woman. At the opening of the front door, the men rose in song for the first hymn. At its end, the friends or acquaintances of the bereaved family would line up in front of the hearse and on the 'off' they would quietly and solemnly walk to the cemetery. The hearse came next, followed possibly by one car carrying the family. Anyone on the road, or those who came out of their houses as the funeral passed to pay their respects, removed any caps or hats and bowed their heads.

At the cemetery there was another eulogy, followed by another hymn. Then the mourners returned to the house for the customary 'ham on plates'. For me, as a boy, the uplifting moment came with the opening of the window curtains, and, after three days of sombre light, daylight streamed in and the atmosphere became the same colour, a much lighter, sunnier shade, even if it was raining.

Most people there were local, but, on occasions, some distant relatives and friends had come from afar, so they were not always recognised immediately. In fact, I once heard of a fellow from Cwmgors who got a reputation for being a professional mourner. Apparently, he'd check in the *Western Mail* newspaper for births, deaths and funeral arrangements and if there was one he felt he could get to he'd turn up, done up in the required outfit, and he'd usually manage the 'ham on plates' at the end because, if no one recognised him, they just thought he was from the other side of the family. The outfit was a stiff, detachable collar, black suit, an overcoat from a wardrobe with a faint whiff of moth-balls about it, possibly a bowler hat, and black shoes. I remember my grandmother reporting from one funeral that a long-lost nephew had turned up from 'up London way', wearing brown shoes. Brown shoes! Outrageous, no shape on him at all, she said.

So many terraced houses in The Valleys had to move the coffin through the window towards the hearse because the internal passageway couldn't be manoeuvred. Indeed, I knew of one area in the Cynon Valley where, if the death had occurred upstairs, the first thing the undertaker did was visit The Temple Bar pub to ask for volunteers amongst the customers in carrying the body downstairs, before rigor mortis set in, because there was a nasty turn in the stairs.

As a side tale, I once attended a funeral in north Wales and, after chatting in Welsh to the mourners in my Carmarthenshire Welsh, I was accorded the honour of being invited to be one of the bearers. My south Wales Welsh must have passed the test, or so I thought, until we got to the cemetery. I was one of the lead bearers and, on reaching the gate, a voice said firmly, in a deep north Wales accent and in north Walian Welsh, 'Turn right.' I didn't think he was talking to me, so I held my ground, trying to carry straight on. The voice rang out again, 'Tell him in English...he's from the south.'

We all have memories of funerals. All personal, but all communal. Everyone followed the formal procedure. There was a template to guide you.

These days, crematoria have entered the formalities and the procedure is, again, usually similar. A chapel or church service first, up to the crem, and then back to a pub or club for the refreshments. There is an extra pressure these days, however...the time slot in the crematorium. I have been in a funeral doing over fifty miles an hour down a motorway to make up time, just to make sure they wouldn't miss their slot.

All ages have their protocol, their set way of doing things. Looking back though, I can't help but feel that the coffin route over the Black Mountain, the exchange of the coffin from the Swansea Valley men, and their Brynaman helpers, on to the Llanddeusant men on the wild, open moorland, had both a certain power and a mental image that reinforced that feeling of the deceased truly being brought home. The cwtch blanket that was laid on that moor, on the cairn hole within the peat bog, gave added power to the whole scene and underlined man's feeling for his fellow man. However arduous the trail, it was the right thing to do.

20. The Western Seaboard

Ceredigion

Sitting Bull, renowned warrior and holy man, famed for defeating Lieutenant Colonel George A. Custer of the 7th Cavalry at the Battle of the Little Big Horn, wasn't actually there.

He was the first leader and chief of the entire Lakota Sioux nation and, together with the Cheyenne and Arapaho tribes, they were the victors at 'Custer's Last Stand'. As a boy he was named Jumping Badger, but bravery in battle got him promotion on the name front.

He had, so it is said, the gift of prophecy and insight and he'd had a spiritual premonition of his most famous victory whilst dancing, chanting, singing and self-harming at a holy rock near the Little Big Horn River. He'd been doing this Sun Dance for days prior to the battle, including fifty sacrificial cuts to his arms, and it had taken a lot out of him. The attacks against Custer on the 25th June 1876 were led by White Bull and Crazy Horse. Sitting Bull was in the camp, guarding the women and children, away from the thick of things. So, at his most famous victory, he wasn't actually present.

I'll tell you a man who was: Sergeant William Batine James, of Pencnwc Farm, Dinas Cross, near Fishguard, virtually across the road from the lane that takes you down to picturesque Cwm yr Eglwys. He was definitely in the thick of things. He was the oldest boy and the sixth of nine children from his farm, hazel eyes, 5' 9" and a Welsh speaker. After his father died, things became difficult on the farm, so instead of heading for the coal mines in The Valleys to seek work, or seeking employment sea-faring, as many men of Ceredigion did, he followed the cry of 'go west, young man'.

He sailed for America in 1870 and ended up driving stagecoaches in Chicago before joining the 7th Cavalry in 1872. He proved an excellent soldier, fighting in various campaigns and being promoted to corporal and then sergeant. He only had a few months to go on his enlistment period when he found himself with Lt. Colonel Custer at the Little Big Horn. He was part of E Platoon, the grey horse platoon. Custer liked to have his platoons on different coloured horses so he could easily pinpoint them in any skirmish.

Most of the cavalry at the battle were killed, including Sgt. William B. James, who died, together with comrades, in the 'Deep Ravine' section of the battlefield, not on 'Last Stand Hill' where Custer met his end.

I had the great privilege of visiting the Little Big Horn battlefield on the 125th Anniversary of the battle, together with the Lakota Sioux, the Cheyenne, a Custer 'look-alike' and incredible re-enactors who were dressed as cavalry and went out on patrol every morning. William's name is on the main monument and adding to the poignancy is the fact that in the Chicago financial centre for the armed forces in America, listed against his name is: 'Savings...40 dollars...unclaimed'.

Looking out to sea from Cwm Eglwys and other seaside hamlets along the northern sweep of Cardigan Bay, so many people fail to appreciate that they are viewing the Welsh Atlantis. Beneath the water lies the submerged Cantre'r Gwaelod, The Lowland Hundred, one of the best-known legends of Wales.

According to the legend, Cante'r Gwaelod was a rich and fertile lowland on which there were sixteen cities, governed by Gwyddno Garanhir, whose palace was apparently near Aberystwyth.

Being below sea level, the area was protected by sea walls and a system of sea level gates under the care of an early version of a civil engineer, or guardian. His name was Seithennyn and he had clearly been appointed in the age old Welsh way of knowing someone on the committee, in fact, the committee chairman, the governor himself, The King. Seithennyn was a man with heavy responsibilities but also weaknesses, intoxicating liquor being one.

One evening, in the fog of a banquet and the heady air of a good night out, Seithennyn forgot to close the sea gates. As luck would have it (and it's always the case, don't you find?), a storm blew up, forcing the high spring tides to break through and flood the entire vast area and causing the people to head for the hills. It was just Seithennyn's luck that a stormy night, high tides and unrestricted booze conspired to cause his downfall, along with his walls.

The tale is recorded in the Black Book of Carmarthen and the manuscript is in safe keeping at the National Library of Wales in Aberystwyth, but when was this catastrophe? Well, at low tide in the village of Borth, a petrified forest can be seen on the beach dated at 1500 B.C., including oak, pine, birch, willow and hazel stumps. South of Borth, along the coastal path to Clarach and Aberyswyth, you can see Sarn Cynfelyn causeway stretching out to sea. At several beaches in Cardigan Bay there are numerous Sarnau, ridges or causeways at right angles to the coast.

In 1770, the Welsh antiquarian scholar William Owen Pughe reported seeing sunken human habitations about four miles off the coast. In 1846, Samuel Lewis reported evidence in *A Topographical Dictionary of Wales* that a collection of stones were visible about seven miles west of Aberystwyth. They were termed Caer Wyddno, 'the fort or palace of Gwyddno'. He also refers to finding stones bearing Latin inscriptions and Roman coins of various emperors at the recess of the tide. Those dates are centuries later than the 1500 B.C. date pinpointed for the petrified trees, but the evidence is real that something happened in this part of Wales, an event so profound and tragic that it remained, remote but recognised, in the deep recesses of Celtic memory, based, it seems, on respected reasoning.

As well as considering the evidence of the petrified trees near Borth and Ynyslas, the fortress stones and causeways, then you must also listen out for the sound of the bells.

When the late evening is still and the breeze is a mere whisper, turn your good ear towards the sea and, if luck is with you and your inner belief is strong, then you might just hear the sound of bells from beneath the waves. The best place is between Ynyslas and Aberdyfi, across the Dyfi estuary, the experience having been immortalised in the folk song 'Clychau Aberdyfi', 'The Bells of Aberdyfi':

Little loves and hope shall fly
Round us in a covey
When we are married, you and I,
At home in Aberdovey.

A new chime of bells was installed in 1936 in the tower of St Peter's Church, Aberdyfi, specifically designed to allow the playing of 'The Bells of Aberdovey'.

Other extensions of the tale of Cantre'r Gwaelod relate to the submergence of the palace of Helig ap Glanwg in the Conwy Estuary. The two stories of Cardigan Bay and the Conwy Estuary could refer to the same legend, separated as the tale has been passed on through the ages. Both refer to the audible sound of bells and ruins visible at certain tide conditions.

So, the wonderment continues. Scientific fact must mould the far off memory of mythology, but all the elements of the story are there. I am a romantic, so I'm going with it... The Lowland Hundred was there and Cantre'r Gwaelod is the lost land of Wales. The next time you are on the coastal belt of Cardigan Bay, look out to sea and, over your flask of tea, unleash your imagination and listen for the bells.

As you sweep northwards along the Bay, take time to take in Aberystwyth, the university town regarded as 'isolated' in terms of access to other centres of sizeable population. It was named in a royal charter in the time of Henry VIII as Ville de Lampadarn, which is worth checking out, but by the time of Elizabeth I, Aberystwyth as a name came into its own. It is a seat of learning, with the National Library of Wales on one hill. Pen Dinas, on another hill, was a Celtic fort. After their invasion, the Normans settled lower in the town, first in their own fortress, built by Gilbert Fitz Richard, grandfather of Richard de Clare (known as Strongbow, for obvious reasons, rather than any cider brewing). Richard's later castle went through several historical experiences, Owain Glyndŵr moving in for a while, and in 1649 parliamentary forces seriously vandalised it.

I can well relate to Aberystwyth being regarded as isolated, especially in my youth. Rugby clubs and rugby playing schools have travelled far and wide on annual tours over the years, to Cornwall, the north of England, even to Europe and the far-flung planetary corners. In my day, the annual 'adventure' was a trip to Aberystwyth. It was a long-haul, stretching into a serious two-day affair by the time the bus collected us after a game and we meandered our way home. It has a sporting tug at my heart, however, in that I only ever scored four tries in my entire sporting life and one of those was in Aberystwyth. Odd thing, I can still remember that light odour of seaweed from the mud of the rugby pitch.

Aberystwyth also had its attractions for our village trip. The front, the pier, the beach, even though it is shingle rather than sandy, the Vale of Rheidol Railway, as one of the Great Little Trains of Wales, Constitution Hill... and Charlie. There is a tradition there that, as a visitor, you should walk the entire promenade and, on reaching the barred railings at the end, kick them for good luck. Constitution Hill has the exciting cliff railway, and a ride on it, even today, evokes warm memories of childhood.

Who was Charlie and why was he so named? He is still there in the Ceredigion Museum: a skeleton, affectionately named Charlie by locals and found in the grounds of the castle, having been buried there in the days of the English

Civil War. The Welsh were dragged into the conflict here, and there, during the various battles and discord.

Travelling north from Aberystwyth you can visit the historic town of Machynlleth with its claim of being the true capital of Wales, having been the seat of Owain Glyndŵr's Welsh Parliament in 1404, and then to the coast again, to Towyn and Aberdyfi. From the town of the famed bells, onwards to Dolgellau, fringing legendary Cadair Idris and still heeding the call of the sea, we head west to Barmouth and then to our next berth, if the sea was only near enough for berthing: Harlech.

The flat land west of Harlech Castle gives the flip side of the tragic Cantre'r Gwaelod extreme flooding experience. During the days of the castle's fortified youth, the sea lapped against the rocks on which the dramatic structure stands. Now, on the land that stretches to the sea, there's a golf course, a comprehensive school and a sizeable community of houses.

This situation is extraordinary, in that the waters of Tremadog Bay, from where Madoc sailed, so they say, to discover America, have receded in the later centuries. Madoc and his men were apparently involved in some serious inter-mingling with a tribe of Americans, producing blue-eyed offspring; an export drive with a difference.

The waters receding conforms with something I heard some years ago, that the whole of the British Isles was developing a tilt. The eastern side, taking in Norfolk, Suffolk and the eastern coastal area was quietly dropping into the sea, whilst the western fringes, Wales included, were rising up to compensate. If this is truly the case, then Cantre'r

Gwaelod, The Low Hundred, will re-appear, giving proof, or otherwise, that it was a large and flourishing inhabited area. It will be a slow revelation, of course, a quick lift-up would be more dramatic and exciting...but overly so for the east of England, lets be fair.

The site of Harlech Castle is spectacular, being one of the formidable links that formed the 'iron ring' circling Wales, ordered by 'Longshanks', Edward I. The views from the battlements towards the sea and Snowdonia are breathtaking. Its magnificent medieval architecture adds to the scenario and fully justifies its status as a World Heritage inscribed site.

Of course, Harlech has been given worldwide profile by the stirring song 'Men of Harlech', which is traditionally said to describe the events during the seven-year-long siege of the castle between 1461 and 1468, and was indeed originally called 'Through Seven Years'. It remains the longest siege in the history of the British Isles. The song has also been associated with an earlier, briefer siege around 1408, which pitted the forces of Owain Gyndŵr against the those of the future Henry V of England. Owain Glyndŵr had, in fact, managed to move in, taking the castle in 1404 and proceeding to hold his Parliament.

A question has arisen over both sieges, in that it has been suggested that there were Welshmen involved on both sides, in attack and defence. It was possibly something similar to the Battle of Culloden in Scotland in 1746, the last battle fought on British soil, when Scotsmen of differing tribes fought on both sides. In some cases, clans were split down the middle. Victory went to the English, with their Scottish supporters, defeat went to the other Scottish Clans, led by Bonnie Prince Charlie, and that put a full stop to his ambitions and the wearing of tartan for quite a while.

'Men of Harlech', as a song and military march, gave an added boost and profile to the vigour of Welshmen when it was used to real effect in two films: *How Green Was My Valley* in 1941 and *Zulu* in 1964. Today it is the slow march for the Welsh Guards and the quick march for the Royal Welsh Regiment. The question remains, to whom does the song truly allude, the defenders of the two sieges or the attackers on the outside, especially if there were Welshmen amongst them? It would be nice to know, just in case it comes up in conversation, at a concert, at a military parade, a trivia quiz, or even during a lull at a whist drive.

Back down the coast for my final lay-by or berthing spot. Just south of New Quay, there is the small, picturesque cove of Cwmtydu. It is also known as Seal Bay, being a popular place for seals to rear their pups. Take care, especially in the months of September and October and if you have dogs, for this seal nursery should have priority and a freedom for the mothers to come ashore to feed their young.

Near the car park you can still see one of the many lime kilns, because, prior to the twentieth century, lime was used to enrich the soil of this largely agricultural area. Lime and limestone blocks were also landed for use in building. A sea landing was, in fair weather at least, the most efficient way of delivering heavy cargo to the coast of Ceredigion.

Cwmtydu, along with other similar inlets and quiet bays, was also a perfect place for the unofficial landings... smuggling. Illegal trading was done with Ireland and the Isle of Man, the latter being very handy because it was not, officially, part of Britain, so ill-gotten gains could be stored there for safe keeping. It was so common and efficient that the total legitimate tax revenue collected hardly covered the wages of the excise men.

The exploits of William Owen of Nevern are legion. He was born to a wealthy family but rebelled against being a normal, law-abiding, God-fearing man. Instead, he set on smuggling expeditions and gun battles at sea, taking his Ceredigion apprenticeship in coastal waters to the seas of the Caribbean, Salamanca and Honduras. His family were no doubt reduced to despair, the law finding itself neutered and even the Good Lord continually reduced to scratching his forehead for inspiration in changing this renegade, to no avail.

Siôn Cwilt was another. He was called 'cwilt' because of the colourful coats he wore, or perhaps the name was a corruption of the Welsh word *gwyllt* (wild). First a local and then a national hero in eighteenth-century Ceredigion, he lived in Synod Inn, where there is still a place known as Banc Siôn Cwilt. He used Cwmtydu and nearby Cei Bach as his workplaces. Armed with sword and pistol, he'd ride his horse to meet the smugglers. Although the authorities chased him, there was considerable support from higher quarters, for the gentry in those parts relied on smuggling to provide restful anesthetics against life's tempests, such as wine and spirits. He was never caught, but some time later in his life a man called Daniel James was caught smuggling and was hanged. Funny thing, Siôn Cwilt disappeared from the scene at exactly the same time.

For me, the most intriguing tale of Cwmtydi is the visit of a German U-boat. Some locals are confused, not that it might or might not be true, but rather, in which World War did it occur...and was it more than once?

Consensus places it in the First World War. The story unfolds to say that a German U-boat entered the cove and surfaced, essentially to re-charge its batteries. According to hearsay, the crew ventured further and a few came ashore to re-stock their supplies, with local butter, eggs, meat, fresh water and beer. Their port of call was the Glanmorllyn Inn, just up the road from the beach. There is a house with that name still there to this day.

Allegedly, the locals, mostly Welsh speaking, accepted the broken English from the visitors as possibly being heavy accents from the English regions. Or, as one pragmatist suggested, in Ceredigion, if there was money to be made...business was business.

One theory put forward was that the U-boat commander knew the area from previous leisurely visits, pre-war. A further cap is put on the story by others, who declared that the crew felt such a warm welcome that one or two re-visited the area some years after the war with their families. I wonder, I just wonder. Were the crew ever there and, if so, was it a question of 'auf wiedersehen, pet' when they left...or to the entire tale itself?

Roy Noble

Roy Noble is a native of Brynaman in the Amman Valley of Carmarthenshire but has lived for over forty years in Aberdare with his wife, Elaine. They have one son, Richard. Roy's early professional career was in education and in the latter years he was a Head Teacher of two primary schools in the County of Powys. He attained bursaries and a scholarship award and was able to travel extensively in Europe and the USA to study education management systems.

His move to broadcasting was gradual and part-time, writing and presenting a weekly 'Letter from Aberdare' on the A.M. radio programme. He eventually joined the BBC full-time and his daily radio programme has attained high listening figures in Wales for a number of years, culminating in a national Sony Award. In television, he attained the Royal Television Society Regional Presenter of the Year Award.

He still broadcasts weekly on BBC Radio Wales and recently completed a Welsh language television series for S4C, touring the Valleys of South Wales on a Honda Goldwing trike.

Roy is a patron and supporter of many charities and organisations and has been the recipient of numerous honours, including the OBE for services to the community and for charity support in Wales.

He has written several books in both Welsh and English and his autobiography, *Noble Ways: Lay-bys in My Life*, was published by Accent Press in 2010.

Graffeg Books

The Most Glorious Prospect:
Garden Visiting In Wales 1639-1900 by Bettina Harden
Hardback, 250 x 250mm, 256 pages, £30.00
ISBN: 9781910862629

The Owl Book by Jane Russ
Hardback, 150 x 150mm, 160 pages, £9.99
ISBN: 9781912050420

Lost Lines of Wales: Bangor to Afon Wen
by Paul Lawton and David Southern
Hardback 150 x 200mm, 64 pages, £8.99
ISBN: 9781912213115

Lost Lines of Wales: Rhyl To Corwen
by Paul Lawton and David Southern
Hardback, 150 x 200mm, 64 pages, £8.99
ISBN: 9781912213108

The Offline Project by Dan Tyte
Paperback, 216 x 138mm, 280 pages, £8.99
ISBN: 9781912213702

A Year In Pembrokeshire
by Jamie Owen and David Wilson
(Publication June 2018)
Hardback, 200 x 200mm, 192 pages, £20.00
ISBN: 9781912213658

Lost Tramways of Wales: Cardiff by Peter Waller
(Publication June 2018)
Hardback, 150 x 200mm, 64 pages, £8.99
ISBN: 9781912213122

Lost Tramways of Wales: North Wales by Peter Waller
(Publication June 2018)
Hardback, 150 x 200mm, 64 pages, £8.99
ISBN: 9781912213139

Lost Tramways of Wales: South Wales and Valleys
by Peter Waller (Publication June 2018)
Hardback, 150 x 200mm, 64 pages, £8.99
ISBN: 9781912213146

Lost Tramways of Wales: Swansea and Mumbles
by Peter Waller (Publication June 2018)
Hardback, 150 x 200mm, 64 pages, £8.99
ISBN: 9781912213153

Mostyn Thomas and The Big Rave
by Richard Williams (Publication October 2018)
Paperback, 216 x 138mm, 224 pages, £8.99
ISBN 9781912654161

For a full list of Graffeg titles and to place an order, please
visit our website: www.graffeg.com.

Graffeg Children's Books

The Pond by Nicola Davies and Cathy Fisher
Hardback, 250 x 250mm, 36 pages, £11.99
ISBN: 9781912050703

The Snow Leopard by Jackie Morris
Hardback, 365 x 270mm, 24 pages, £17.99
ISBN: 9781912050475

The Ice Bear by Jackie Morris
Hardback, 365 x 270mm, 24 pages, £17.99
ISBN: 9781912050468

Bertram Likes To Sew by Karin Celestine
Hardback, 150 x 150mm, 48 pages, £6.99
ISBN: 9781912213610

The Very Silly Dog by Nick Cope
Paperback, 150 x 150mm, 48 pages, £4.99
ISBN: 9781912213511

No I Don't Wanna Do That by Nick Cope
Paperback, 150 x 150mm, 48 pages, £4.99
ISBN: 9781912213535

For a full list of Graffeg children's titles and to place an
order, please visit our website: www.graffeg.com.